ArT RANDOM

KYOTO SHOIN

First published in Japan 1989 by KYOTO SHOIN INTERNATIONAL Co., Ltd.
Sanjo-agaru, Horikawa, Nakagyo-ku, Kyoto, Japan. TEL[075]841-9123

Editorial director : Kyoichi Tsuzuki
Art director : Ichiro Miyagawa
Editorial coordinators : Edit deAk, Midori Nishizawa

ISBN4-7636-8543-0 C0371 P1980E

Printed and bound in Kyoto by SHASHIN KAGAKU Co., Ltd.

Translation : Fia, Inc.

cover : The Elizabethan Phrasing of the Late Albert Ayler / The Armitage Ballet
photo by Gianfranco Gorgoni

A-T RANDOM

Karole Armitage and David Salle

3 Years of The Ballet Stage

Dance into Paintings / Paintings that Dance
Peter Schjeldahl

The Elizabethan Phrasing of the Late Albert Ayler is work of large ambition undertaken, like the whole collaborative project of Karole Armitage and David Salle, in the teeth of daunting social, cultural, and economic obstacles. For both better and worse--better in terms of broad significance, worse because confusing--Ayler is an event in the grand integration of pictorial and theatrical aesthetics that has been a persistent artistic striving in both Europe and the U.S. for about a decade. It is an occasion for reflecting on the exciting possibilities and also on the discouraging difficulties of such striving in a world ill-prepared to comprehend it. The difficulties, in particular, are full of import for the present fate of Western high culture. Unless confronted, they will also muffle our pleasure in the glories of Ayler.

Just how hard a thing Armitage and Salle are trying was impressed on me, in a small but telling way, at the New York premiere in May 1986 of their first realized piece, The Mollino Room (with Mikhail Baryshnikov and The American Ballet Theatre), at the Metropolitan Opera. The glittering ballet audience responded hesitantly, with some murmurs of protest, to the work which was sandwiched on the program between rivals of a 1908 Fokine and a 1949 Balanchine. (The regular ballet critics, as their reviews would prove, were likewise discomfited.) The section of invited art-world types where I sat--most of us friends of Salle--were predictably more enthusiastic, but an odd thing happened to it at intermission: some people left. They had applauded Armitage but were indifferent to the prospect of a work by Balanchine, the greatest choreographer of this century and, incidentally, a particular object of Armitage's emulation and rivalry. Seats left empty by painting aficionados (quickly taken by young ballet aficionados with standing-room tickets), no less than the general audience's disaffection, showed what Armitage and Salle are up against.

The collaboration of an advanced choreographer like Armitage and an advanced pictorial artist like Salle may roughly double the constituency for each, but the level of understanding in this expanded audience, relative to the work, will be drastically reduced. Such is the specialization of knowledge and taste today that almost no one will have an equal grasp on the choreographic and the pictorial issues of a really sophisticated collaboration. Even with the best of will -- hardly to be assumed when devotes of one art are often perfect philistines when it comes to other arts -- almost anyone's response will be partial and eccentric. This being inescapably the case, might it be, somehow, okay? As an art professional and dance amateur writing about a largely choreographic work, I prefer to think so. Otherwise, humility about my own partial, eccentric viewpoint would shut me up. I propose that humility--awkwardness, even embarrassment--is appropriate and fertile ground for an approach to The Elizabethan Phrasing of the Late Albert Ayler. It is the personal site of cultural lack, the absence of an audience combining deep knowledge of both painting and dance with a radical temperament, an appetite for transformations. I hazard, further, that this ideal, non-existent audience is the true subject (in both senses) of the Armitage/Salle enterprise. The Elizabethan Phrasing of the Late Albert Ayler's initial impression of violent disjuncture and miscellaneousness intensifies the pleasure, which is a delightful sense of mastering, through sheerly aesthetic perception, apparent chaos.

Trying to get a handle on my own delight, I am remembering, now, The Mollino Room and my first inklings of what Armitage and Salle were up to. Much about the piece eluded me completely, but a couple of things made me feel suddenly privy to a marvelous secret logic. The first was the shockingly simple, almost insolent way Armitage used Baryshnikov: strictly as himself, the star and perfect dancing machine. Choreographed separately from the other eight dancers, with whom he never interacted (as if the stage were a double-exposed film of dances taking place at different times), he was quite gratuitously run through the gamut of his incredible technical repertoire. Armitage thus coldly bracketed a virtuosity developed to serve expressive ends. (Deprived of such ends, the ballet critics seemed literally not to notice the awesome display.) Therefore, we in the audience were not to lose ourselves in the ballet, but we were to see ballet dancing--of the highest imaginable quality, in this case--employed as simply an element in a theatrical thing being made before our eyes.

My other moment of revelation in The Mollino Room concerned a recorded comedy routine, from the early '60s, by Mike Nichols and Elaine May, used to accompany a slow, intricate, adagio duet of male and female dancers. (The entire rest of the piece was accompanied by austere Hindemith music.) The routine--or the shambles of a routine, since Nichols and May (their era's most sophisticated comics) were reduced to helpless giggling by the silliness of the material--involved a Jewish son revealing to his mother, who rapturously surmises he will become a doctor, that he plans to become a nurse. In conjunction with a tense, erotic pas de deux on stage, the recording triggered, for me, delirious reflections on the mystery of collaboration: what it means and entails to make a thing (a joke, an art work, sex, anything) with another. The almost frightening amplified laughter of Nichols and May--laughing at themselves, at how funny it is to want to be funny--was like a noise from some subterranean chamber in creativity's castle. The ballet critics hated it. One called the recording a vile insult to male nurses! Yet another--an erstwhile avant-gardist--said The Mollino Room placed

Armitage and Salle "in the civil realm of the reactionary," meaning I suppose that they ought to be arrested.

In essence, I think they trash the pieties both of ballet form and of pictorial form by subordinating them to each other. They make dance into picturs and make pictures dance. Like an alarm clock, the pictorial in a piece like Ayler shatters the dream-time of dance: even the choice of music or voice accompaniment feels "picturesque." Meanwhile, choreographic rhythms destroy the integrity of the stage picture, splintering visual contemplation. The disruption is far more radical than in any previous picture-making dance theater I've seen, from Merce Cunningham/Robert Rauchenberg to Robert Wilson or Pina Bausch: however odd or disparate the elements composed by those artists, they remain within an essentially unchanging, though unfolding, tableau. In Armitage/Salle, on the contrary, each image and passage makes a jagged break with what preceeded it and even with what is simultaneous. We must, indeed, keep waking up, freshly alert to each thing in turn. There is no possible half-way response for anyone who pays attention.

With all this in mind, I will talk about Ayler, mentioning only a few aspects and elements of that vastly complex work. Approaching it critically, I have a particular feeling familiar to me from the several times I have written about David Salle's paintings: that there is no end of things to investigate or say but also no certainty that any particular investigation or statement will be really helpful or necessary. In general, the only use of knowing the formal and iconographic background of elements in Ayler, as in Salle's paintings, is to be relieved of wondering about it. Certainly, in years of learning the sources of Salle's imagery I don't feel I have, by that means, enhanced my sense of the work's "meaning" very much--the meaning being a function of my visual, emotional, visceral experience. Everything germane to that experience is right on the surface of the work. With Ayler, similarly, the real trick for understanding is simply to believe one's eyes and ears: one sees and hears precisely everything one needs to know.

Armitage's dancing in Ayler matches the hard working sprightliness of Lord Buckley's style, which is a kind of strenuous projection of looseness: "hip," "crazy," and "groovy" stylizations of freakish mental states. She moves with jerks and pops that make glyphs of "cool," "frantic" feeling. It's like a parody of a parody of a "modern dancer", but totally under control. Armitage makes spectacular use of her drawing-in-space-sculpture of a body. (She sometimes seems to have five or six elbows.) the dim lighting, with a glow around her, is wonderfully spooky. The overall poetic suggestion is something like this: we have plunged directly into the profundity of the psyche, and what do we discover there? Style, purely superficial expression, as startling as a splash of cold water. I'm reminded of another thought I had about the big eye drop: that it was a sign telling me what to do, which was "Look!" Meaning look at the "look", the appearance, of things. Look, don't think. That's how you get what Ayler has to give.

At the end of the first part, Armitage is rewarded for her dance--that's how it feels--with a big jeweled ring that descends from the flies. Come to think of it, Ayler is full of big images of small things: ring, eye, lightbulbs, gumball machine, Dutch-type painting (a sea battle), and so on. The scale effect is to dwarf the dancers, making them feel smaller-than-small--as if they could indeed fit inside a head or in, say, a Faberge egg. Anyway, the ring is a highly "romantic" image. One of the dancers told me she thought it was about how Salle feels about Armitage, giving her this big ring--but they are "classicists," as they keep reminding us, and not romantic autobiographers. I think the ring is more an exaggerated image of "romanticism" itself, a way of introducing the subject of ballet. All ballet is mainly about erotic feelings, right? And Ayler turns out to be, among other things, a fiesta of erotic appearances and gestures: many versions of maleness and femaleness, some silly and some perverse and some genuinely sexy.

Mostly, passages tumble into each other. I have the impression that this drives normal ballet audiences crazy. They want indications of what's coming and, when it's over, of what just happened, and Armitage won't oblige. Whatever's occurring at the moment is made sharply clear, though, in the Balanchine way. The point is that you have to take the dancing as it comes. If you try to think back or ahead, you get lost.

Armitage's duets are absolutely her best stuff, I think. In Ayler, they are where the extreme contrast of masculine and feminine pays off, making for excruciating erotic tension. It's very impressive, even a bit scary, to experience this tension that is based entirely on artificial dance impressions. The dancers have no consistent characters--they change character almost from minute to minute!--and there is no narrative, or rather there is so much narrative, so many torn scraps of story-like-ness, that it amounts to the same thing. So we merely see dancers performing sequences of moves abstractly suggestive of love or hate, menace, self-absorption, desire, dependence, surrender, violence, whatever, all completely cool and objective. And yet the intimacy of it, in terms of my feelings when I watched (no doubt from the summoning of my own blissful or horrible erotic memories), just about killed me at certain moments. This is the payoff for a total aesthetic investment in surface, appearance, look, style. Once you are absorbed on that level, the simplest canny manipulation of an image can effect you like a heart attack. Right before the end, Ayler, hits a plateau of harmonious erotic feeling--powerful and free, as serene as a bird gliding on extended wings--that I want to call "courtly."

Theater is a medium that exists very largely in and for talk--banter exchanged with acquaintances in lobbies, rumination shared with friends over late night suppers. It's what theater is about for me, in terms of making me feel part of a civilization not yet defunct. Admittedly, theater talk is a very faint component of this era's noise, but the test is quality rather than quantity: quality of passion, timbre of wit. By trying to constellate a new audience, Armitage and Salle are in effect attempting to focus and elevate theater talk, making it more aesthetically serious, less socially parochial, and more fun. The lovely sound of it, or its lack, will tell us whether or not they are succeeding.

舞踏と絵画(抄)

『亡きアルバート・アイラーのエリザベス風フレーズ』は、キャロル・アーミテージとデヴィッド・サーレが厳しい社会的、文化的、経済的障害に抗して取り組んだ野心作のひとつである。良しにつけ悪しきにつけ——広い意味での重要性では良きものであり、混乱しがちな点では悪しきものではあるが——『アイラーの…』は、この10年間ヨーロッパ、合衆国双方において執拗に試みられてきた芸術的努力である、絵画美と劇場美の統合にかかわるイヴェントといえる。

アーミテージのような優れた振付け師とサーレのような優れた画家による共同制作を観に来る人間の数は、それぞれの客の倍にはなるだろうが、こうして多く集まった客の理解度は、大幅に低くなることだろう。知識や嗜好の専門化がこんなにも進んでいる今日、真に洗練された共同制作における、振り付けと絵画とを同程度に理解できる人間はいないのではないか。

それは各人の文化的な欠落であり、絵画および舞踏に関する深い知識と、変化を求める欲求とをうまく結合できる観客がいないということでもある。さらに言えば、この理想的で実在しない観客こそ、アーミテージ／サーレの真の主体である。

本質的には、彼らはバレエのフォルムと絵画のフォルムとを相互に従属させることで、両者のもつ敬虔さを破壊しているように思う。舞踏を絵画化し、絵画を踊らせるのだ。『アイラーの…』のような作品における絵画的な特質は、古き良き時代の舞踏を打ち砕く。音楽や声の選択でさえも「絵画的」な感じがするし、いっぽう振り付けのリズムは舞台を熟視することをさまたげ、舞台全体の統一性を破壊してしまう。それぞれのイメージとパッセージは前のイメージやパッセージ、あるいは同時進行中のそれとはまったく異なる際立った変化を見せていく。観客は一瞬も舞台から注意をそらすことができないのである。

『アイラーの…』におけるアーミテージの舞踏は、抑制を解かれた力の反映であり異常な精神状態の様式化であり、モダン・ダンサーのパロディーのパロディーのようにみえて完全にコントロールされたものである。アーミテージは肉体の、空間彫刻のドローイングともいうべき使いかたが素晴しいのだ。ほの暗い照明の中でダンサーにスポットを当てた舞台は幽霊でも出そうにわくわくする雰囲気で、詩的に表現するならば、我々は魂の深奥にまっさかさまに落ちてしまう。そこにはなにがあるのだろう。スタイル、純粋に表層的な表現、冷水の飛沫のように人を驚かせるものである。巨大な眼の背景について考えていたことを思いだす。つまり、それは私になにをすべきかを教えてくれるサイン、すなわち「見よ！」だ。「見よ」、物の外観を見よという意味である。見よ、考えるな。そのように我々は『アイラーの…』が提示するものを受け取るのである。

種々のパッセージは相互にぶつかり合い、普通のバレエ・ファンは混乱をきたす。いま起きたことの次になにが起こり、それがいつ終わるのかをファンははっきりさせて欲しがるものだが、アーミテージはおかまいなしである。舞踏を、登場するがままに受け入れねばならないということが重要である。後戻りしたり先走って考えようとすると、わからなくなってしまうのだ。

アーミテージのデュエットは最高の作品である。『アイラーの…』ではエロティックな緊張感を取り入れなかったかわりに、このデュエットが男らしさと女らしさの極限のコントラストを表現している。演技であるこのような舞踏からこれほどの緊張感を経験するのは少々恐しくもあるが、しかし感動的である。ダンサーたちには一定の役がない——ほとんど瞬間毎に役を変える——そして物語もまったくない、いや、むしろ非常に多くの物語があるのだが、あまりにたくさん断片として存在するため最終的には同一化してしまうのだ。つまり我々は愛、憎しみ、脅威、自己陶酔、欲望、依存、降服、暴動など、クールで客観的な事柄を抽象的に示す動作をダンサーが連続的に演じるのを見るにすぎない。私には（明らかに我が至福の、あるいは恐るべきエロティックな記憶を呼び起こして）これに覚えがあるという思いで、ほとんど死にそうになるときがあった。これこそが表層、外観、外見、スタイルに投じてきた美的投資全部への報いなのだ。いったんこのレベルに没入してしまうと、単純かつ巧妙なイメージの操作が、心臓発作のようにあなたを襲う。『アイラーの…』の幕切れ直前に、調和の取れたエロティックな感覚の状態——力強く自由で、羽を広げてすうっと飛んでいく鳥のように落ち着いた状態——私はこれを「雅(みやび)」と名付けたいのだが、そのような状態が訪れるのである。

劇場は、非常に広い意味で会話によって、また会話のために存在する空間である。夜食をとりながら友人と熟考を分かちあい、知り合いとロビーでおしゃべりを交わし…いまだ滅んでいない文明の一部を感じさせてくれるという意味から言うと、それが私にとっての劇場のなんたるかである。劇場での会話は現代の雑音の非常に微々たる要素でしかないとしても、吟味されるべきは量ではなく質である。情熱の質、ウイットの特質である。新しい観客を集めようとすることによって、アーミテージとサーレは、実のところ劇場での会話に焦点を当て、それを高めよう、審美的により真摯で社会的な偏狭を排し、もっと楽しめるものにしようと試みているのである。劇場での楽しい会話のざわめきがあるかないかによって、彼らの成功、不成功を知ることができるであろう。

ペーター・シュジェルダール

THE MOLLINO ROOM

Created for American Ballet Theatre

Premiere : April 10, 1986
John F. Kennedy Center for the Performing Arts Washington, D.C.

Choreography: Karole Armitage
Scenery and Costumes: David Salle
Lighting: Jennifer Tipton

Music: Paul Hindemith
Conductor: Paul Connelly
Dialogue : Mike Nichols and Elaine May

FIRST MOVEMENT

Paul Hindemith's Kammermusik
No. 5 Concerto for Viola and Orchestra, First Movement

SECOND MOVEMENT

Nichols' and May's dialogue, My Son the Nurse

THIRD MOVEMENT

Hindemith's Quartet No.3, Op. 22, Third Movement

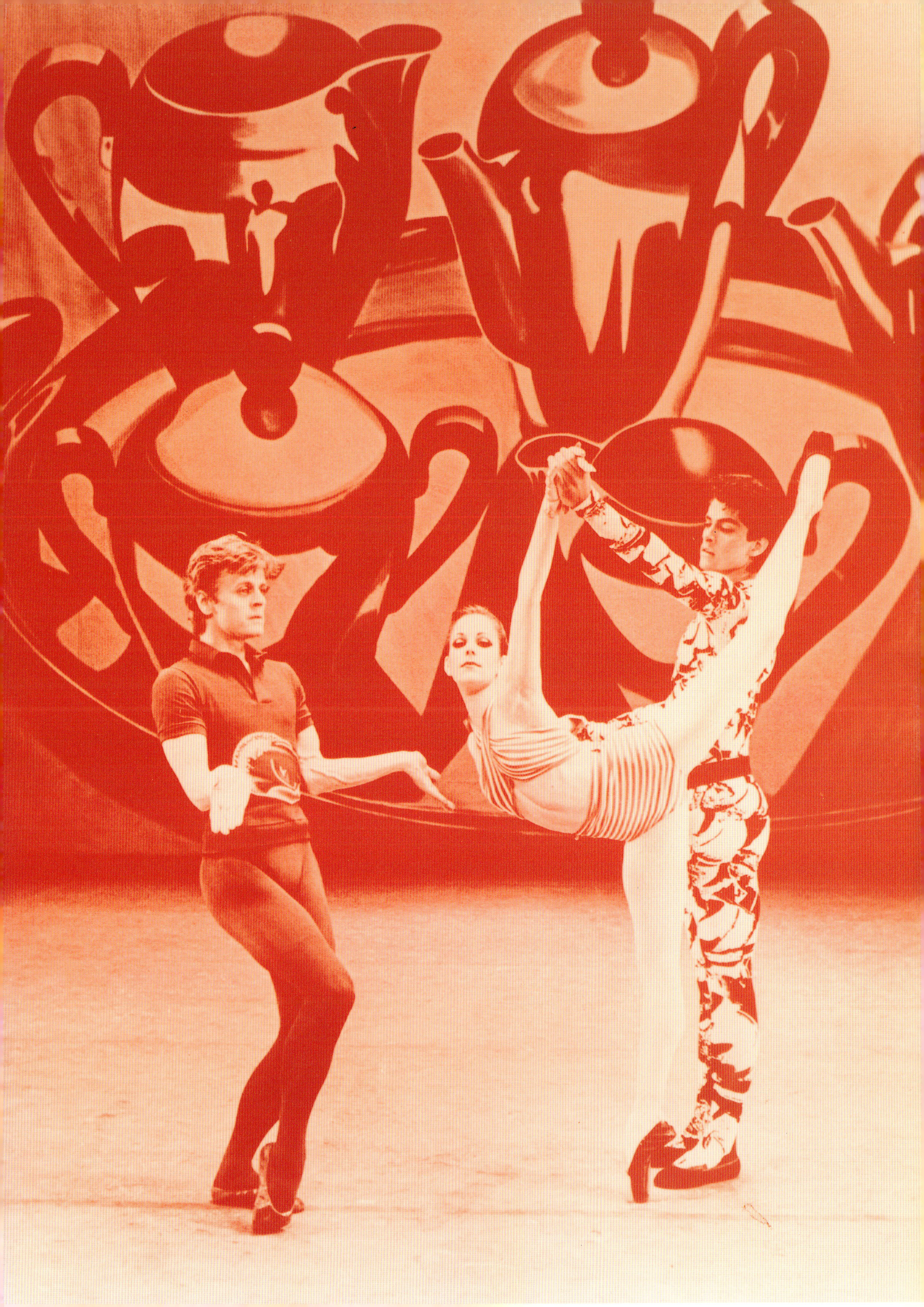

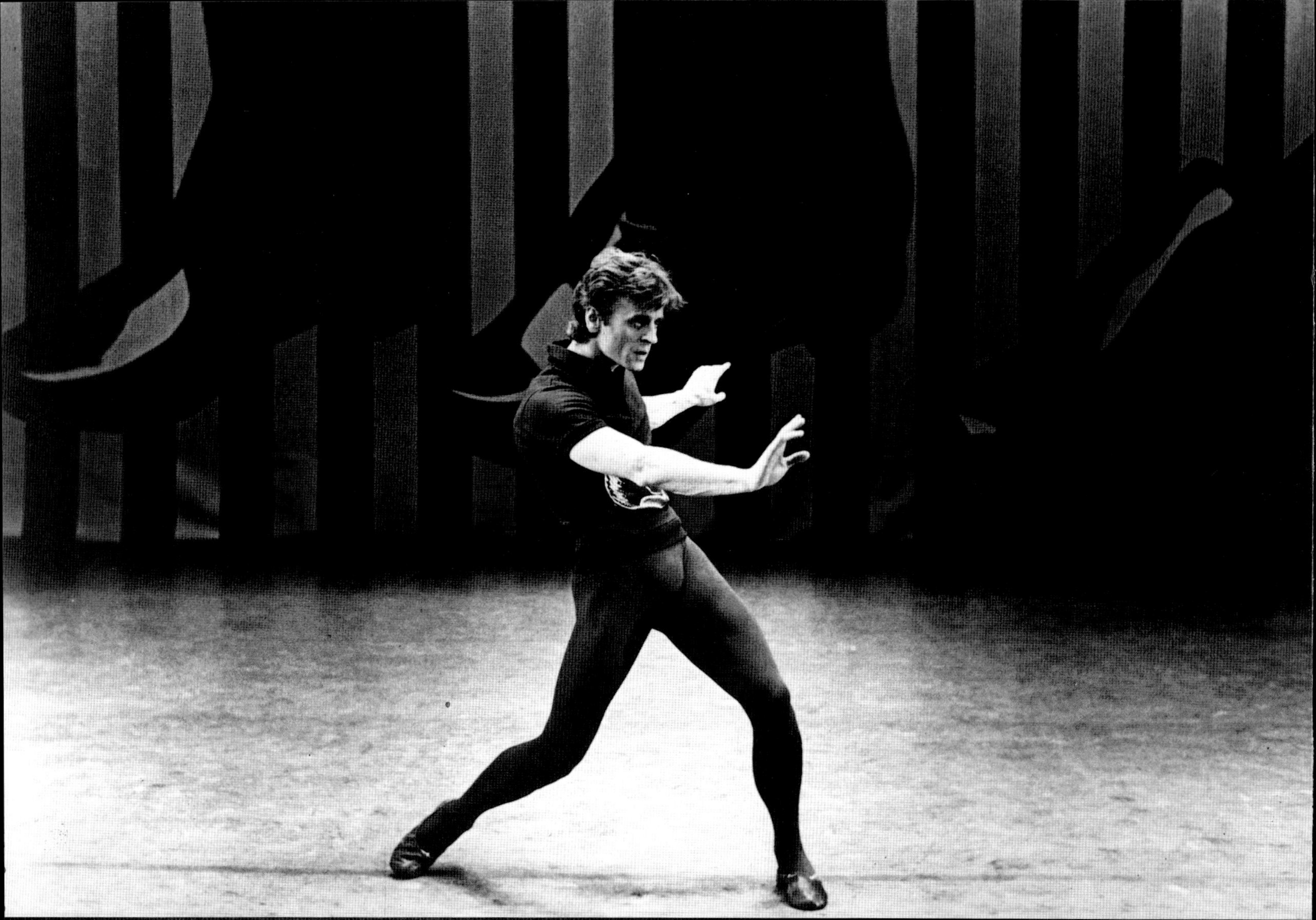

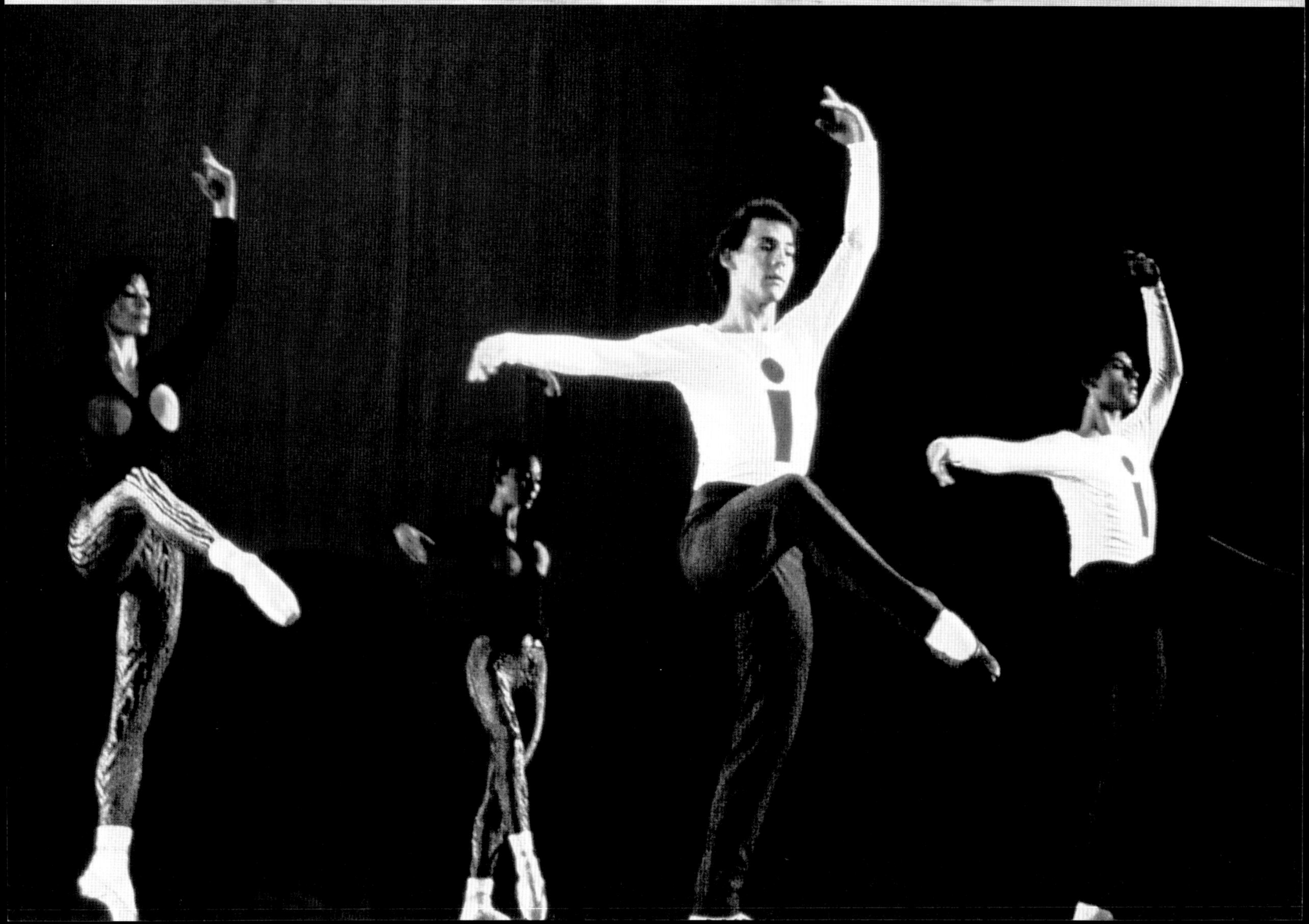

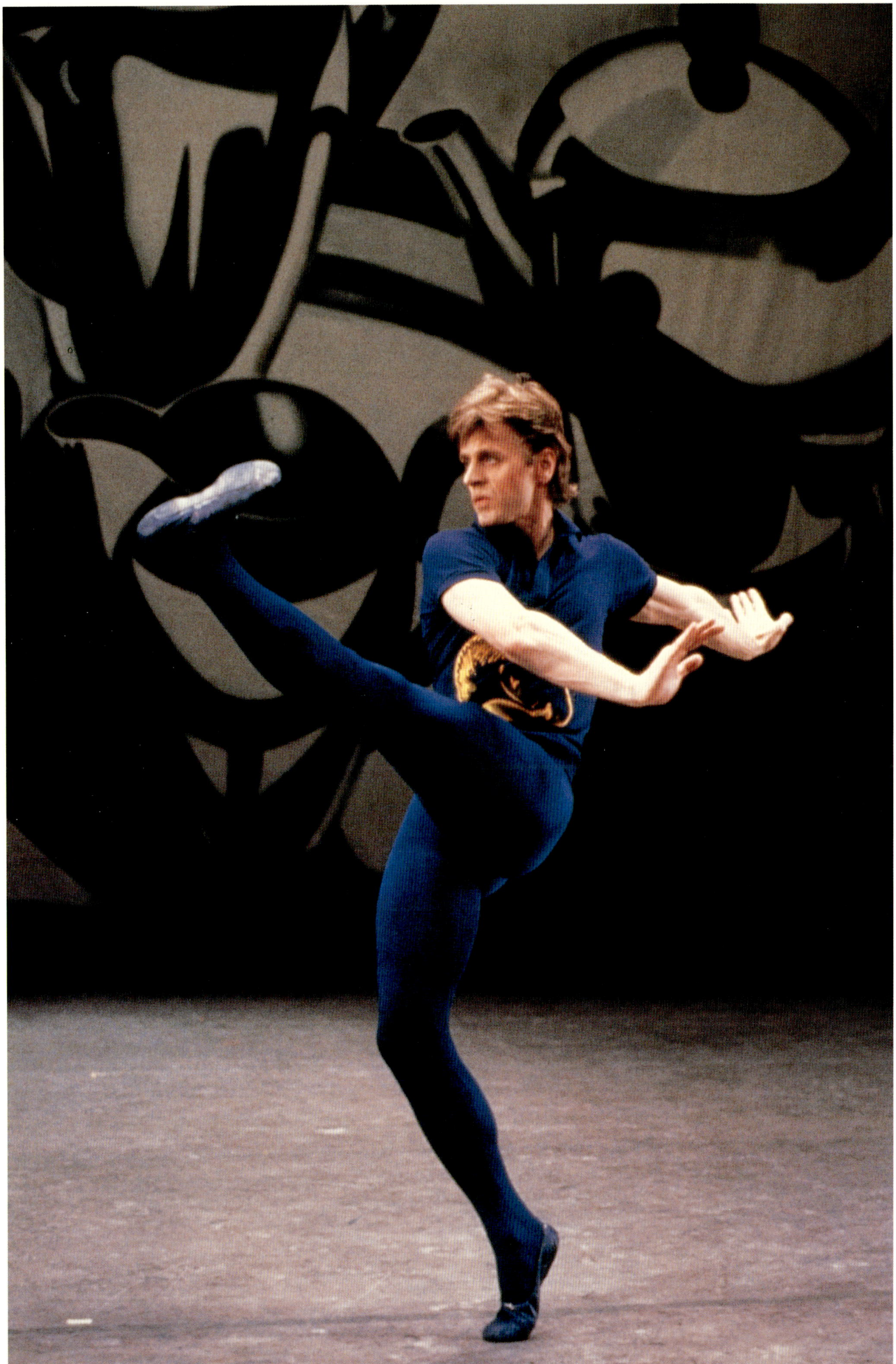

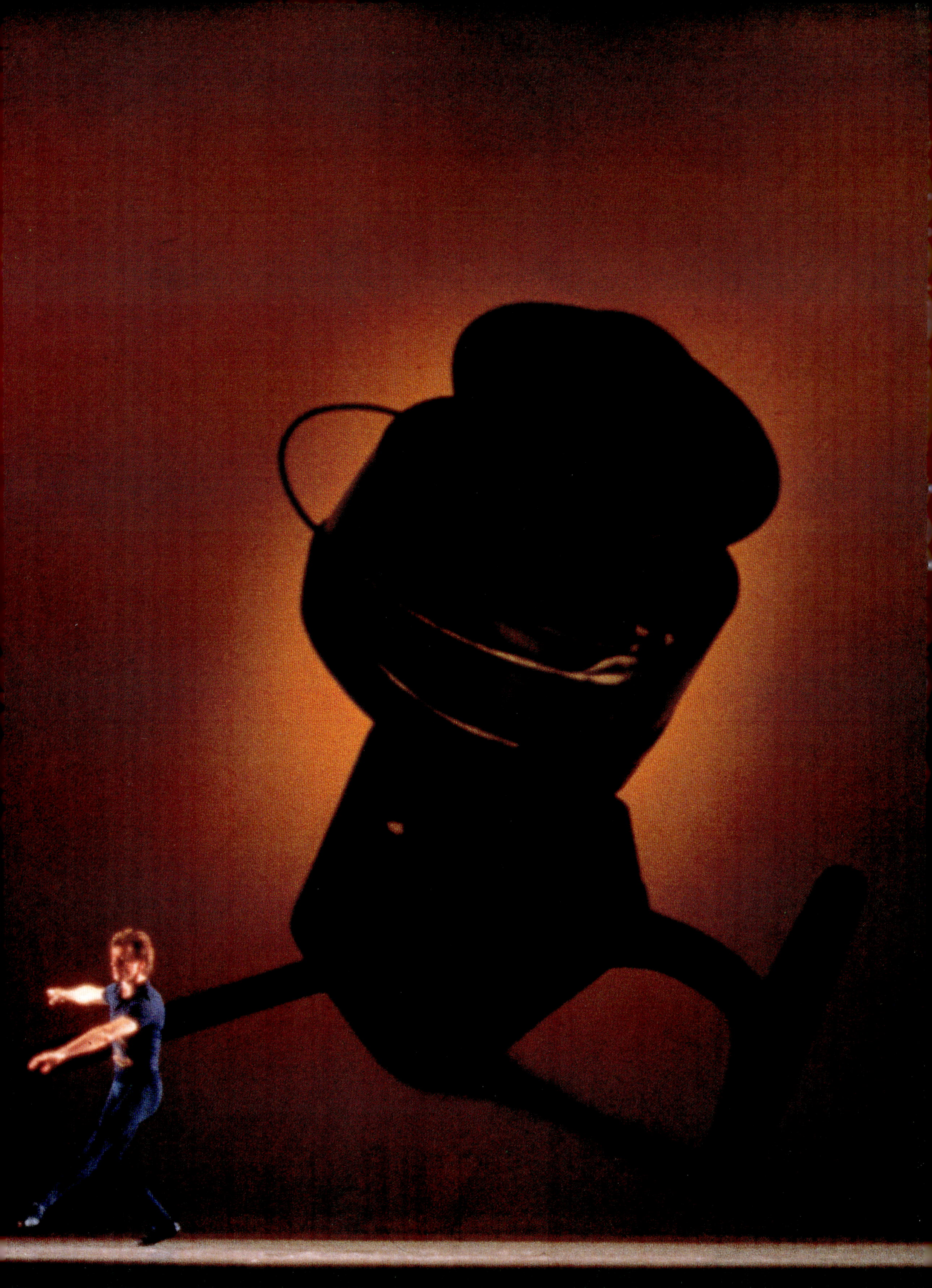

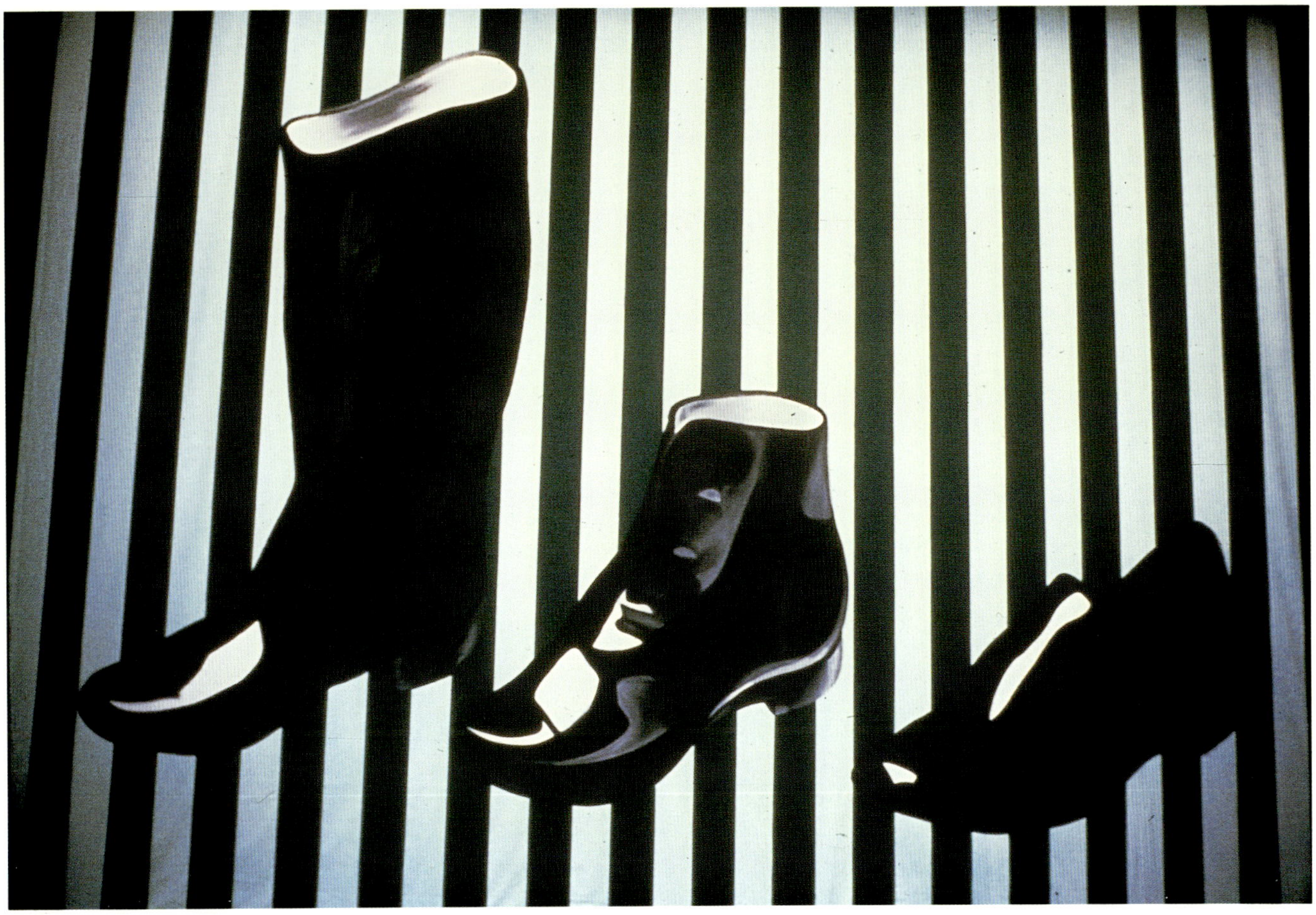

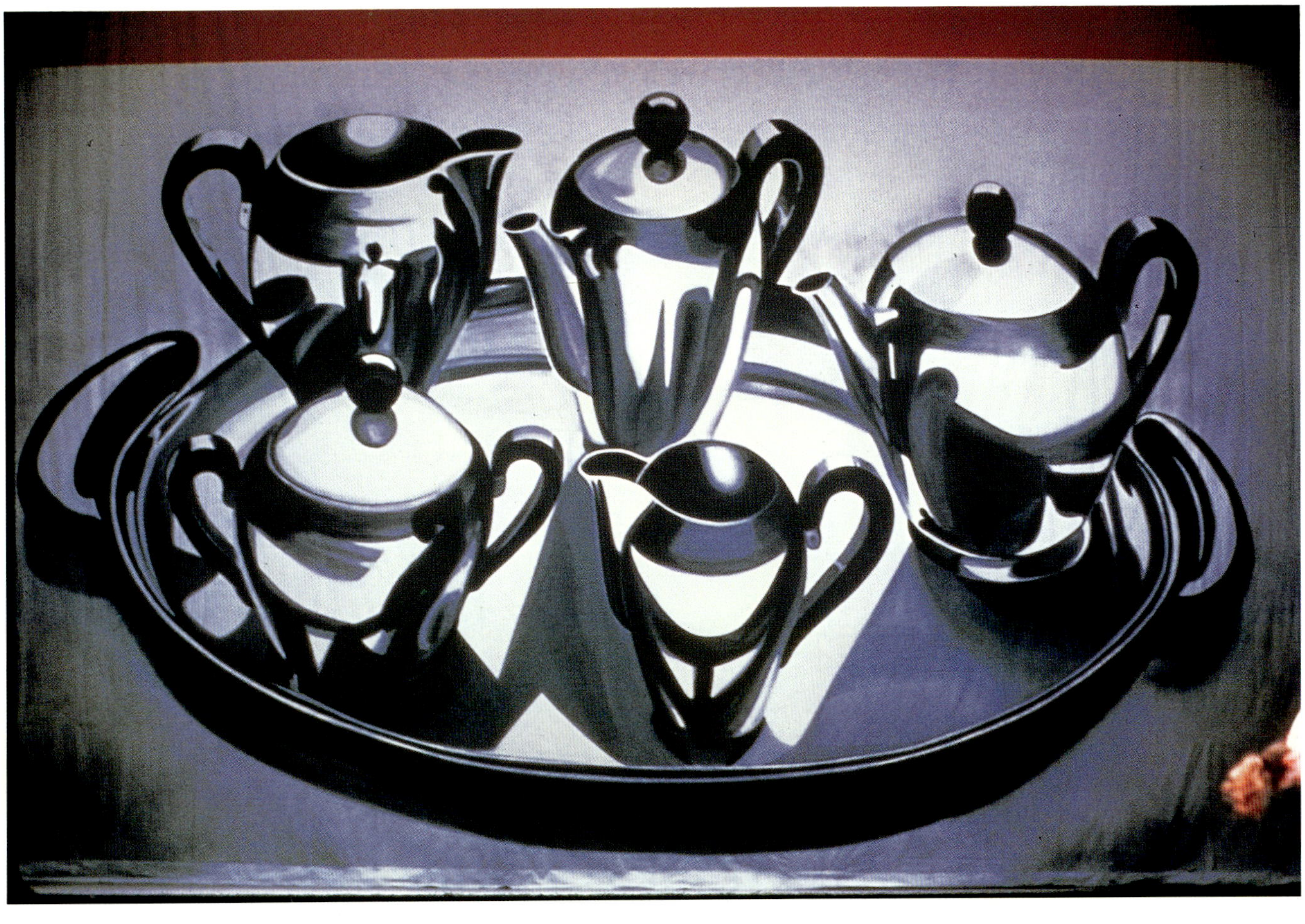

THE ELIZABETHAN PHRASING OF THE LATE ALBERT AYLER

Armitage Ballet Premiere: September 25, 1986, Eindhoven, Holland

Choreography : Karole Armitage
Scenery and Costumes : David Salle
Lighting : Ken Tabachnick

Music
ACT I

Subconscious Mind....................................... Lord Buckley

Funf Satze Fur Streichorchester.................... Anton Webern
Pierre Boulez conducting the London Symphony Orchestra

Sakura, Sakura...Yo-Yo Ma
Michio Mamiya, arranger and conductor

Marc Antony's Funeral Oration.................... Lord Buckley

Three Pieces for String Quartet.................... Igor Stravinsky

ACT II

Bells... Albert Ayler

Our Prayer.. Don Ayler

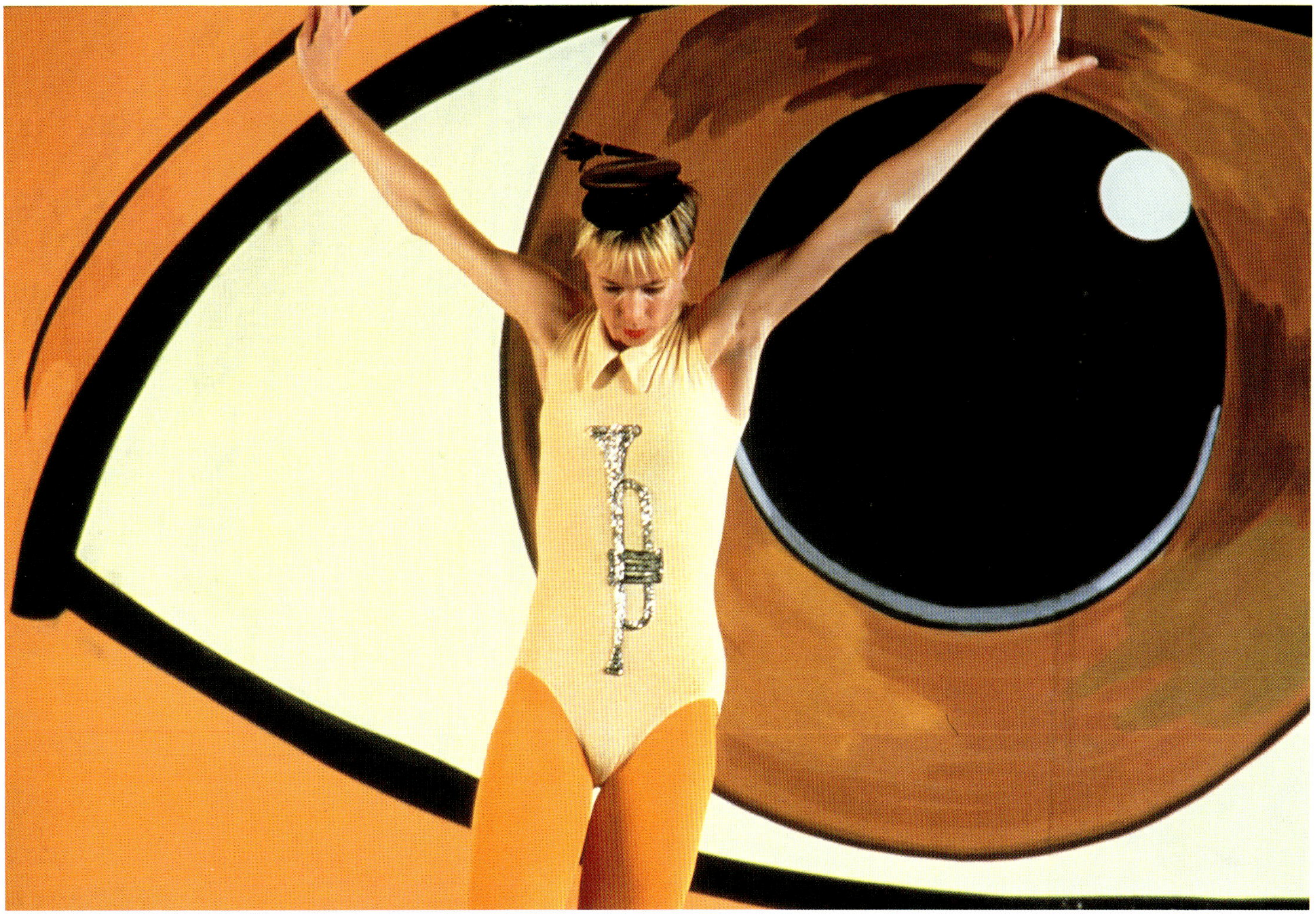

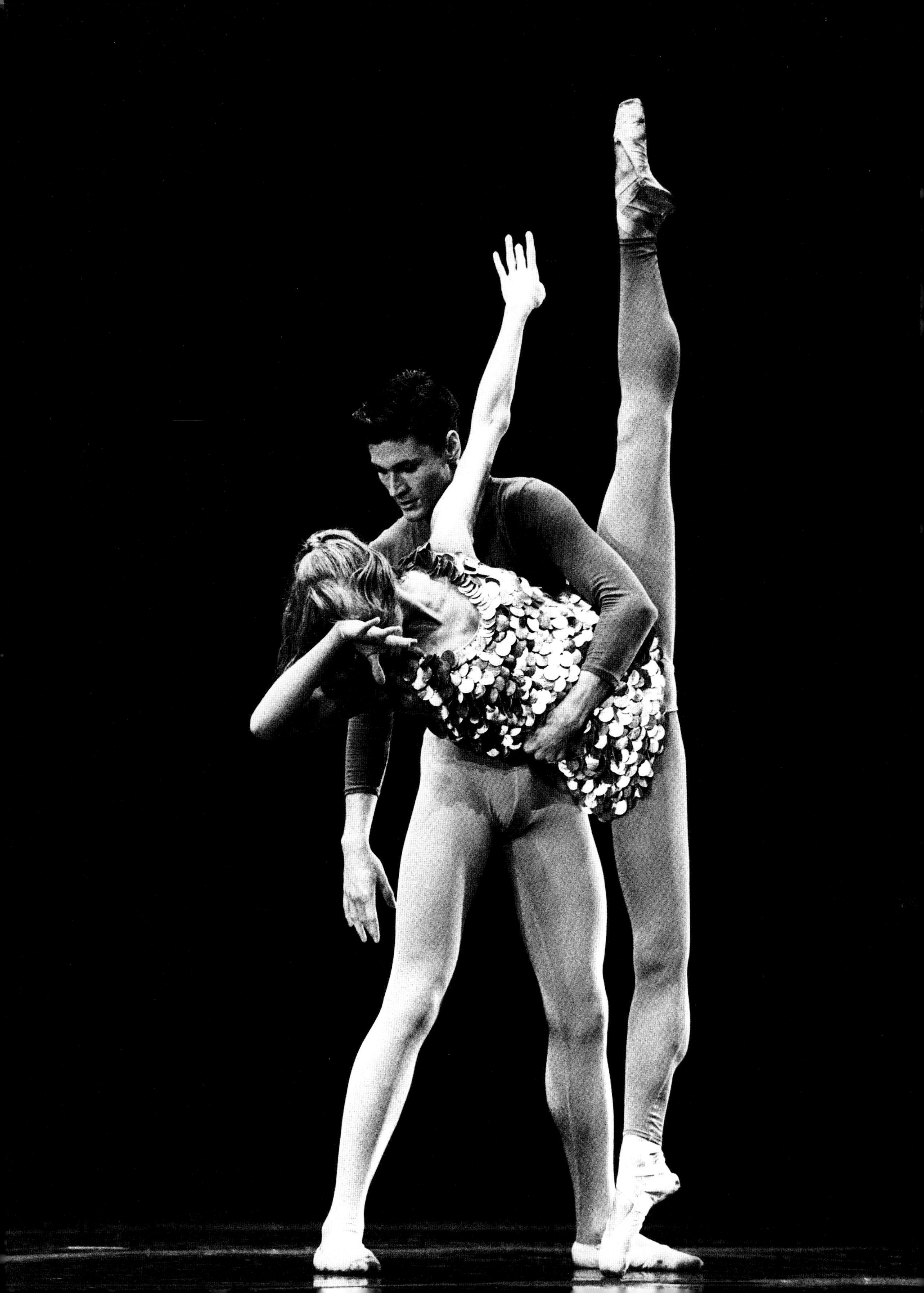

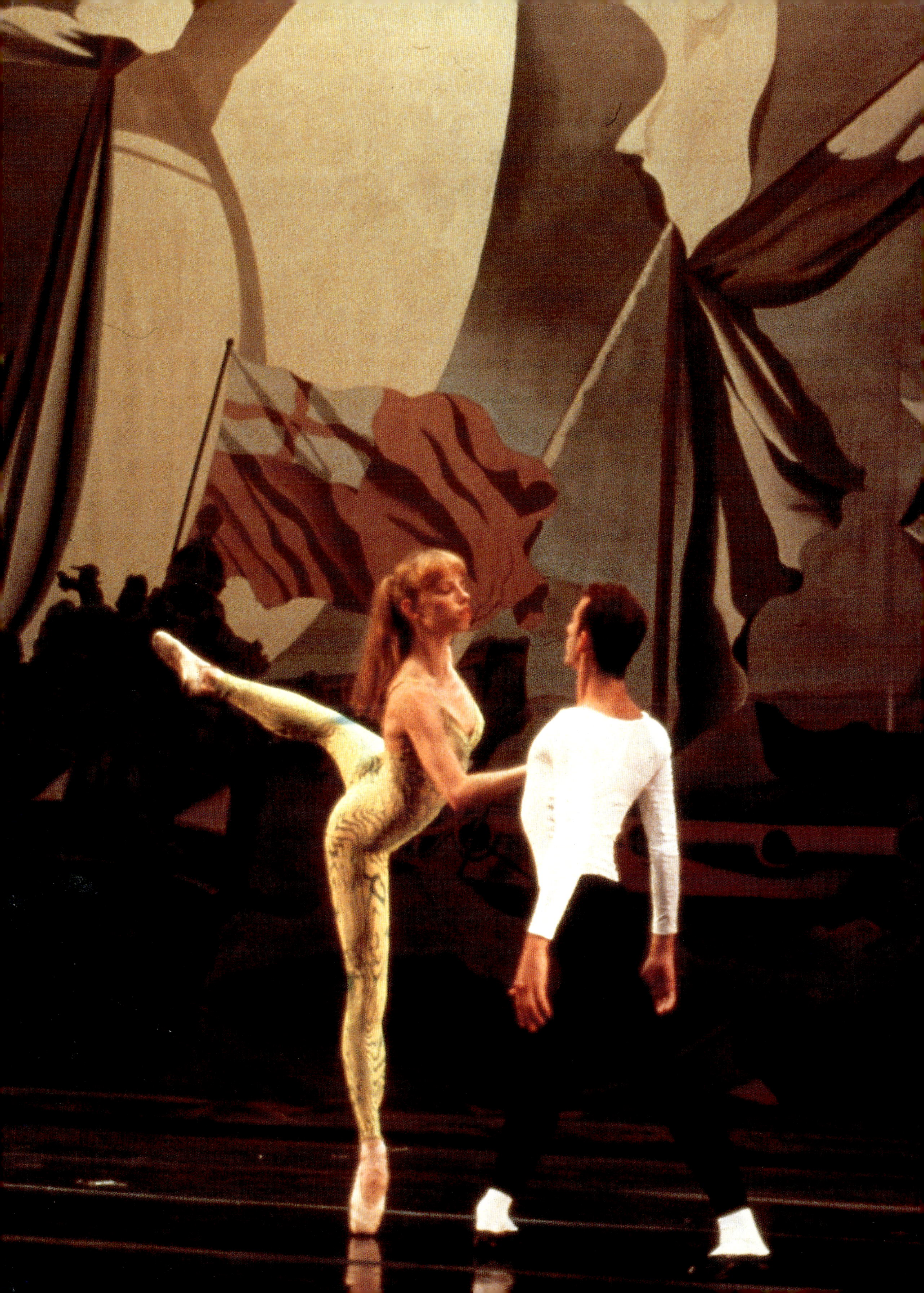

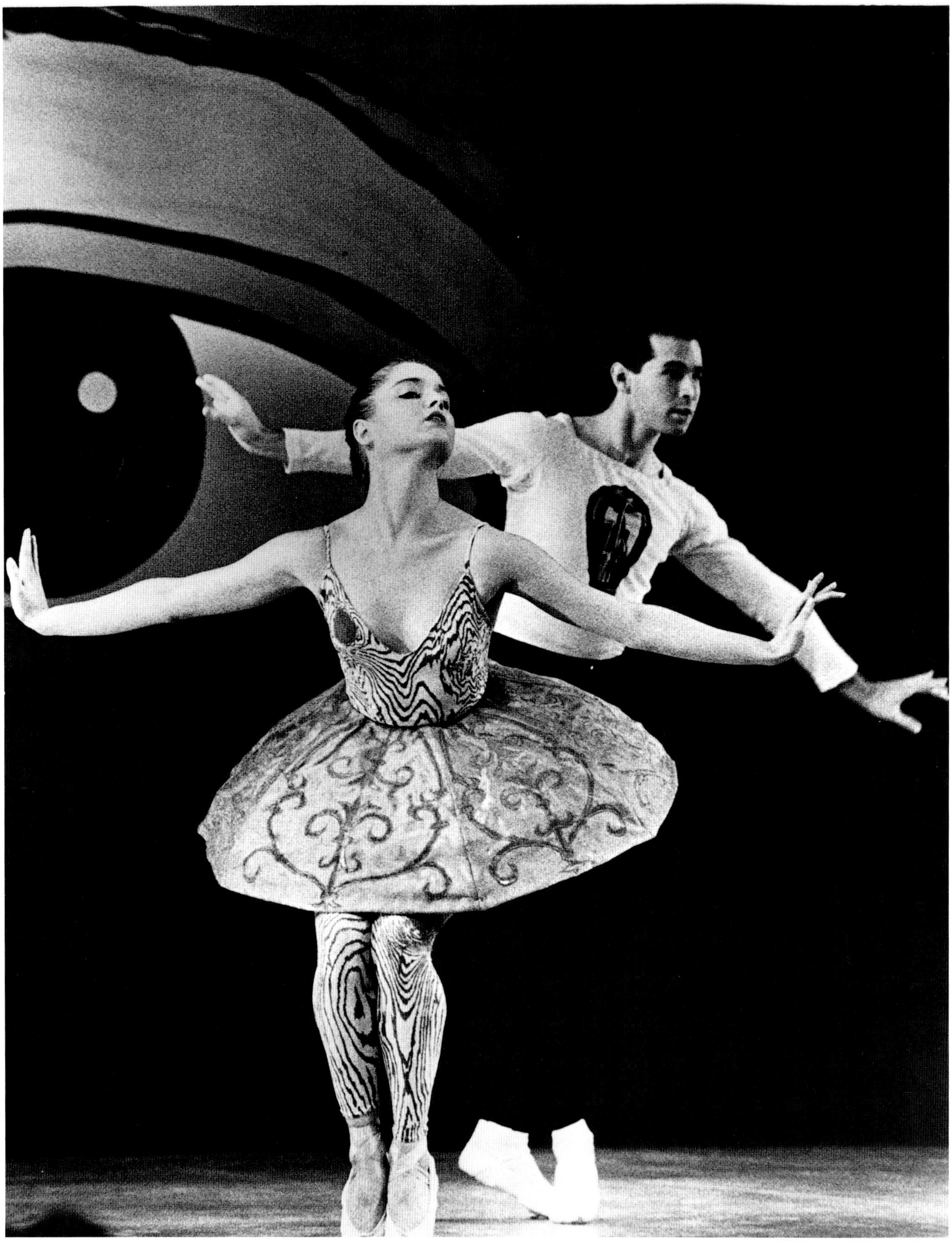

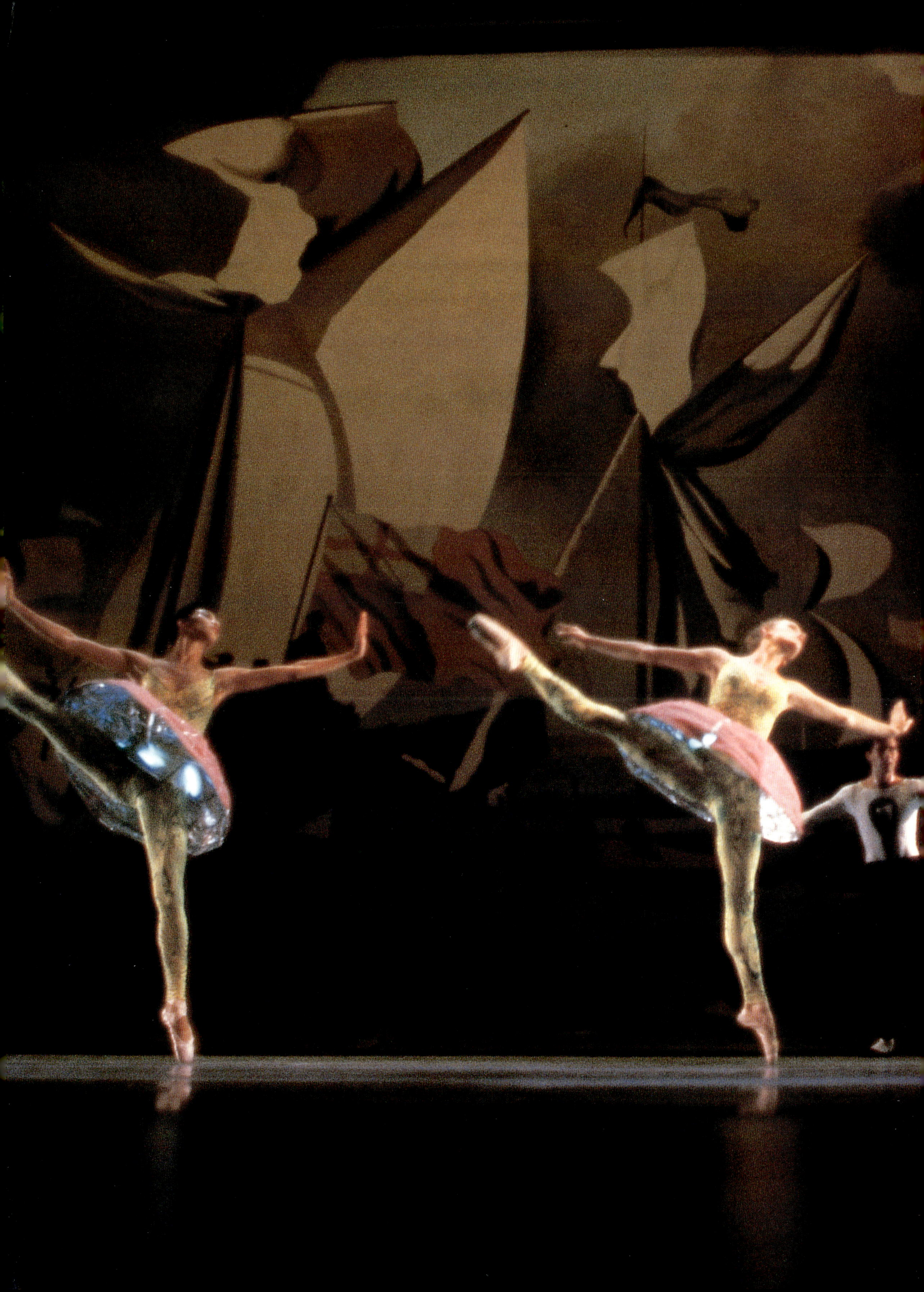

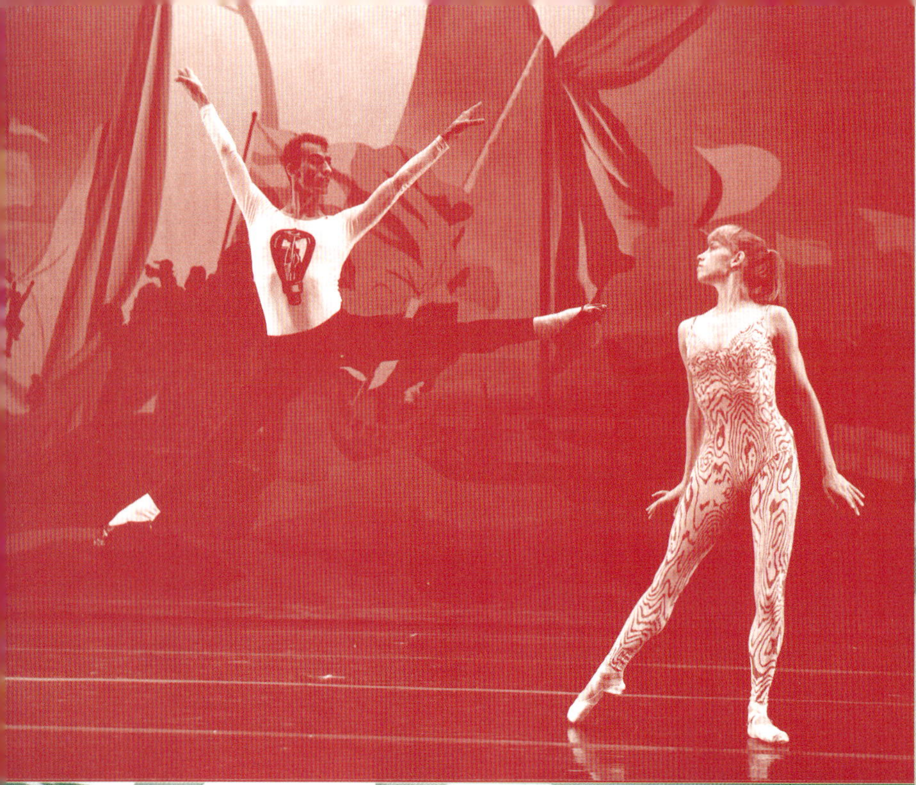
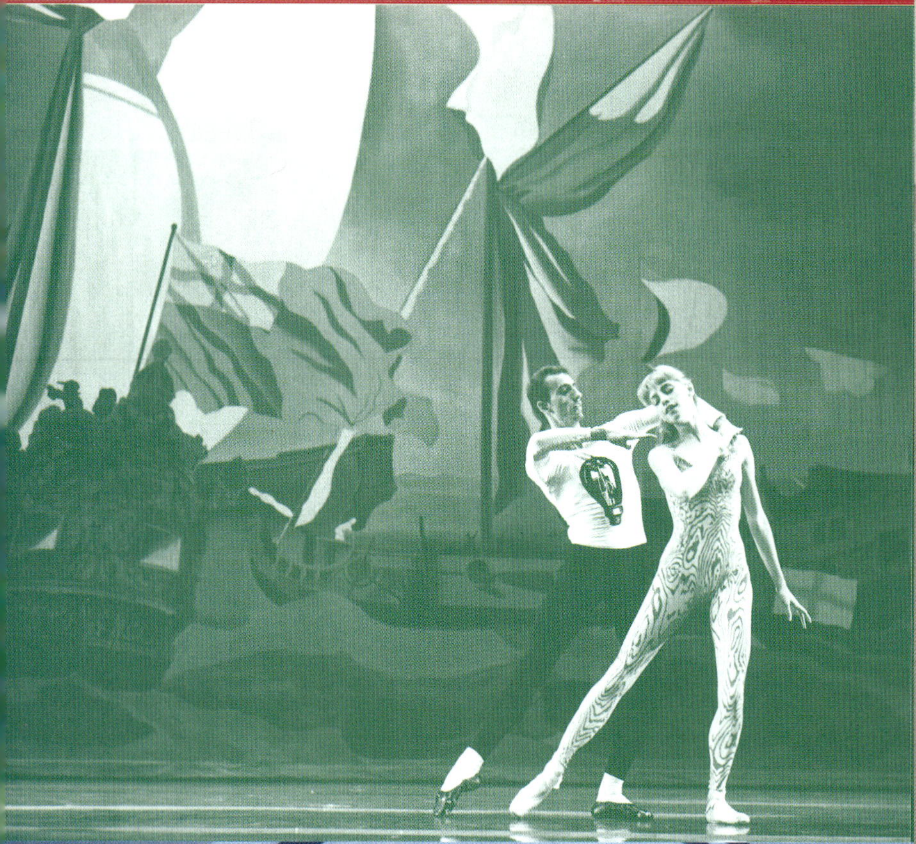
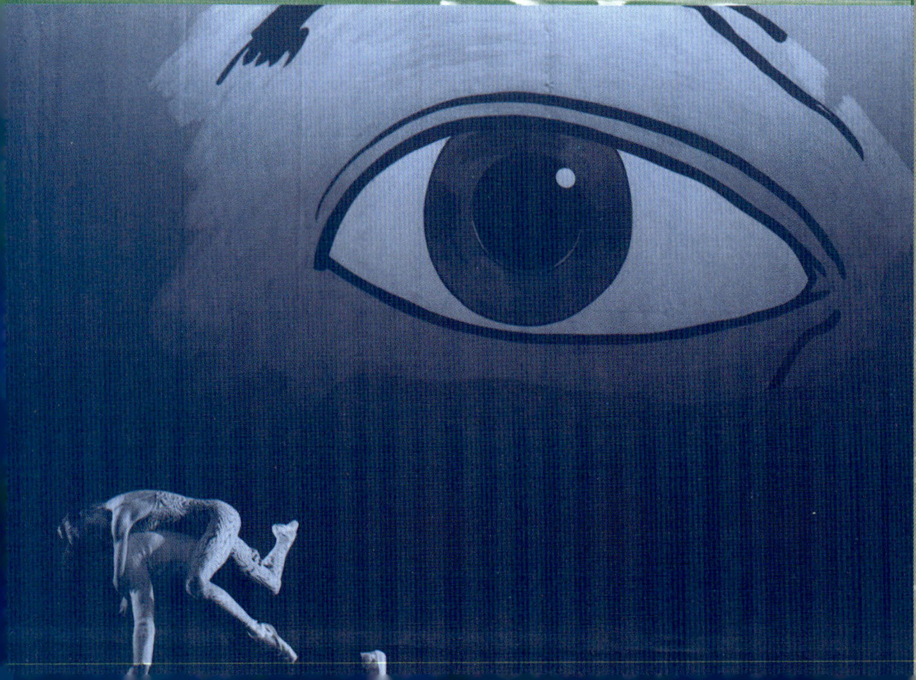
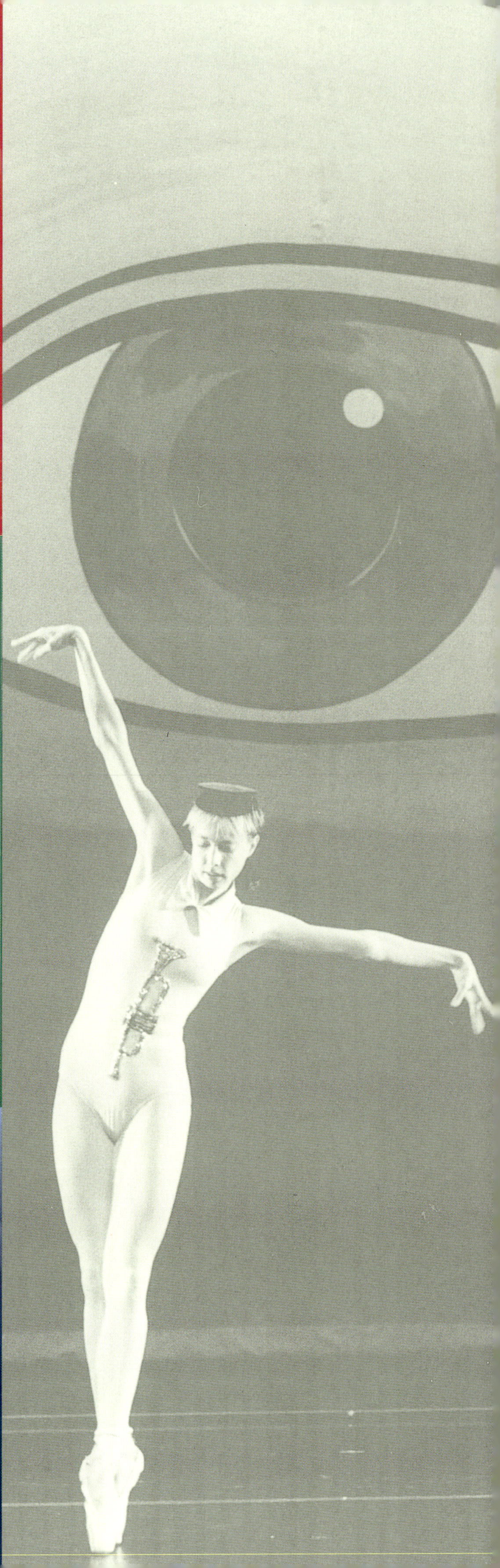

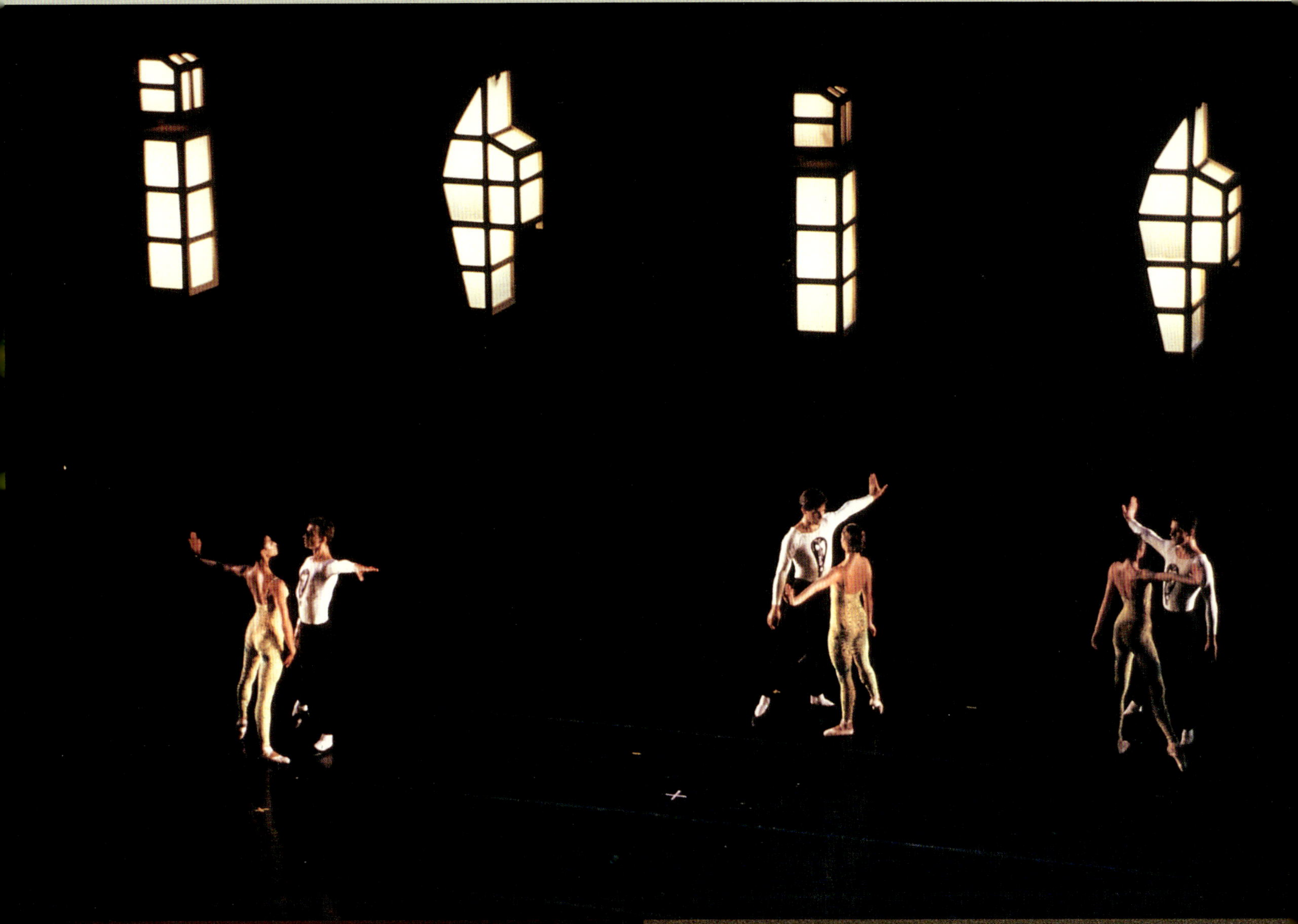

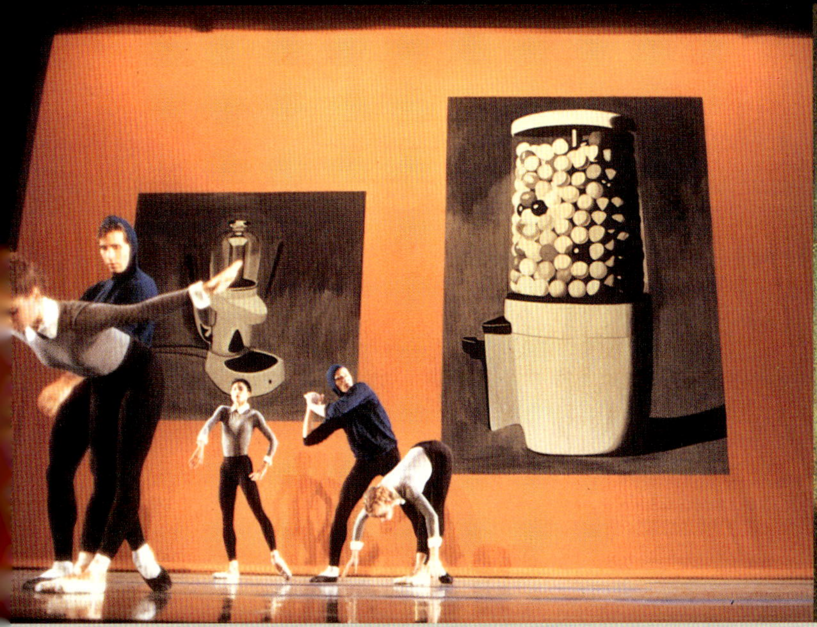

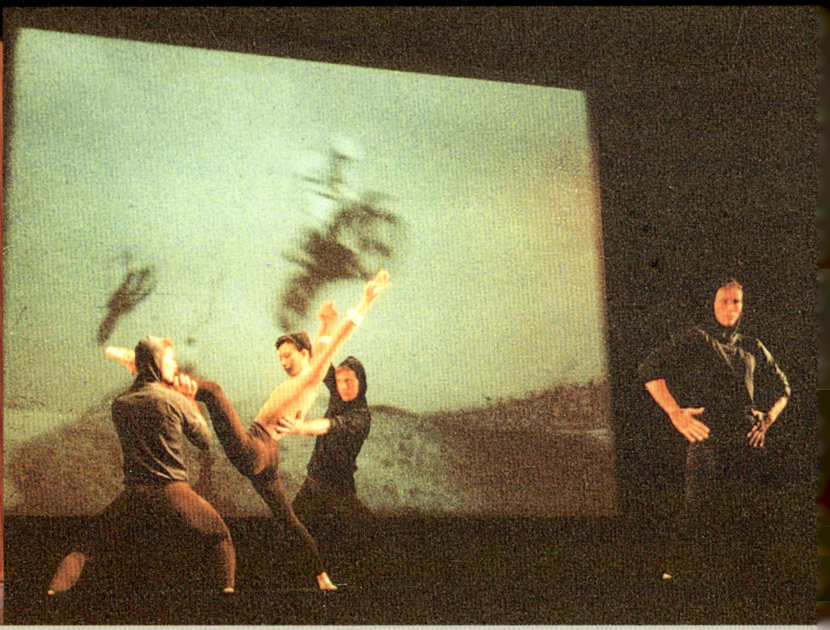

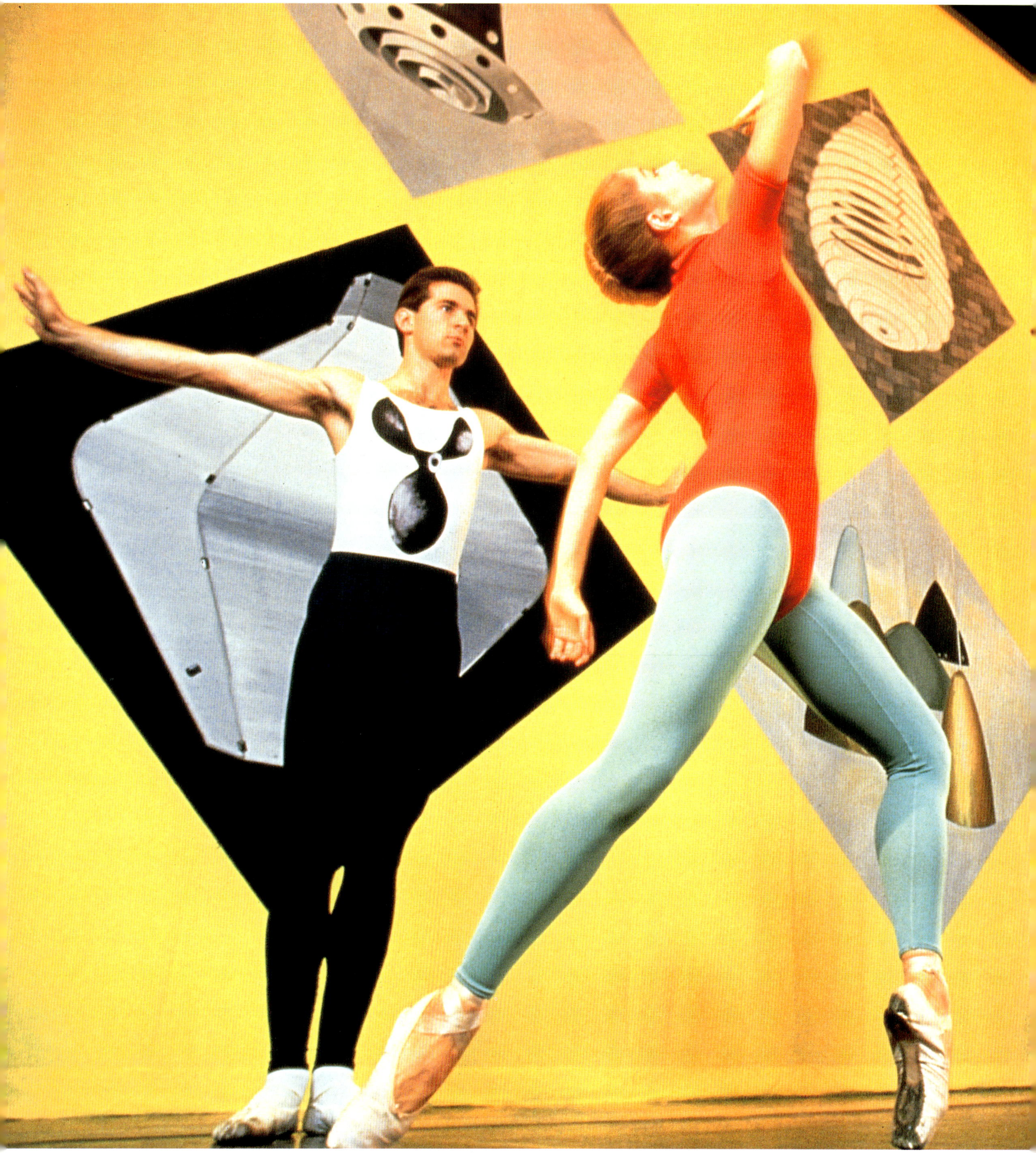

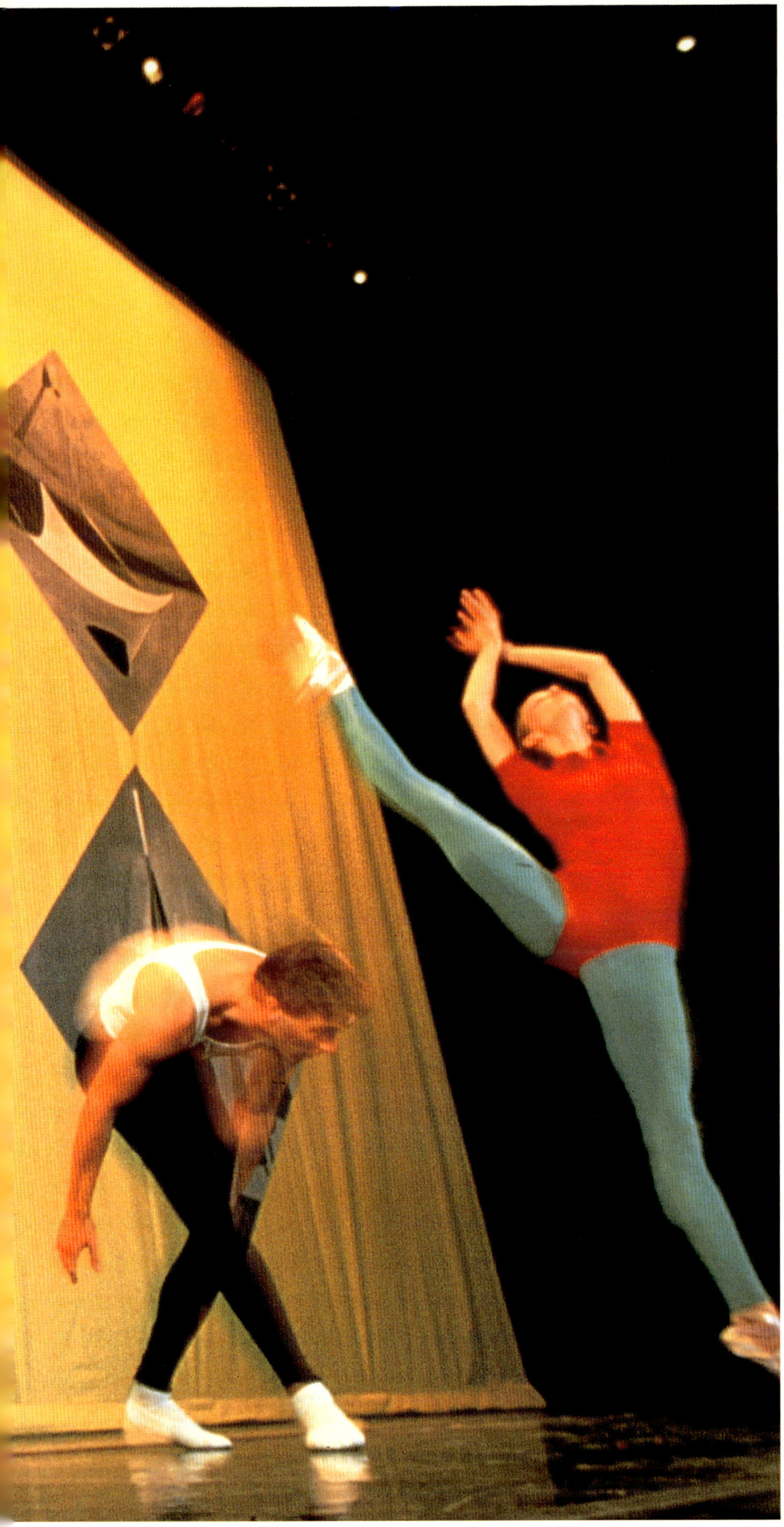
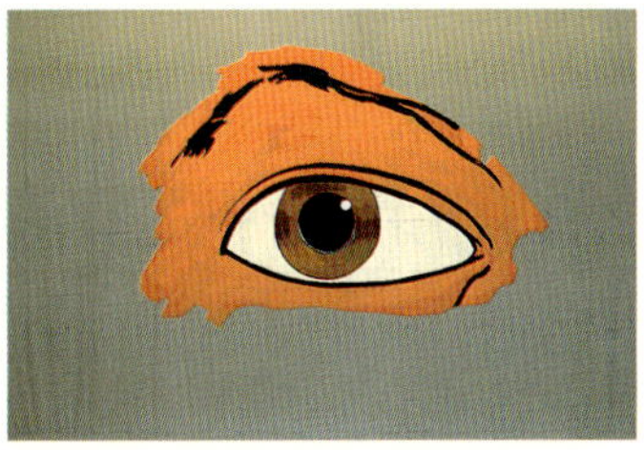
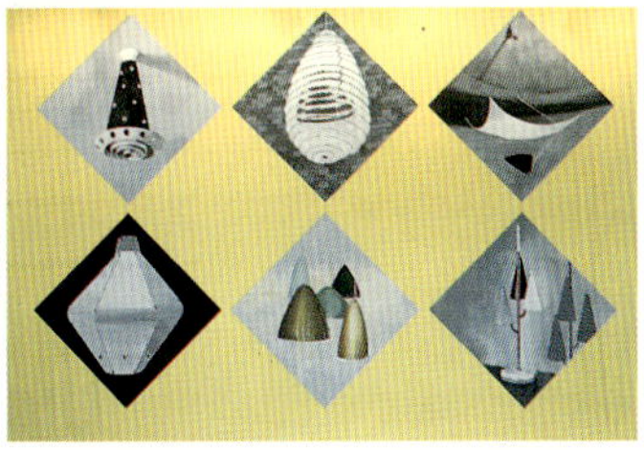
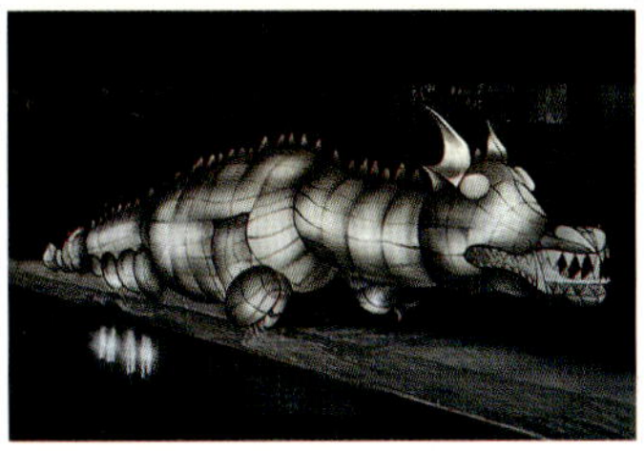
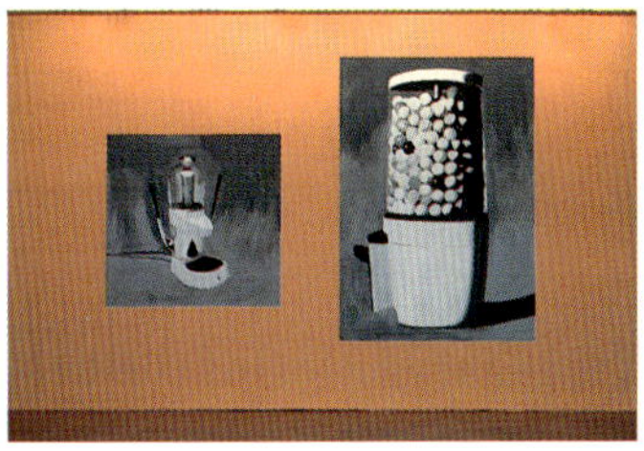
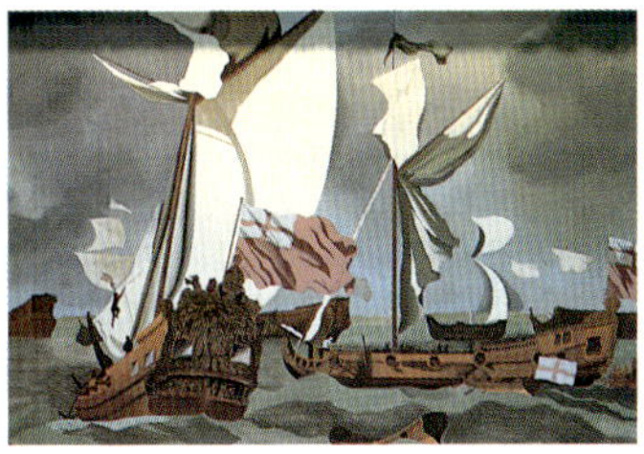
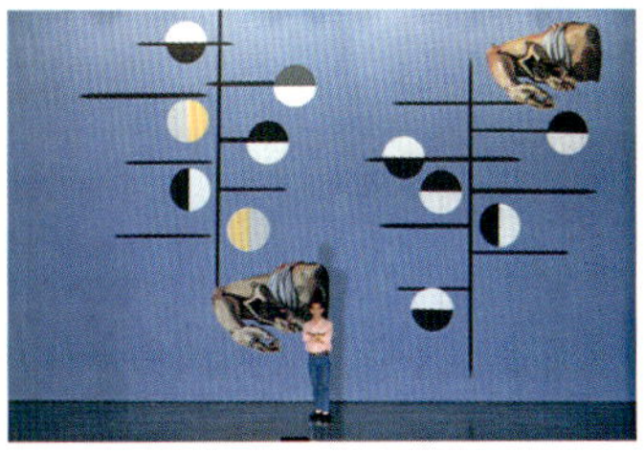
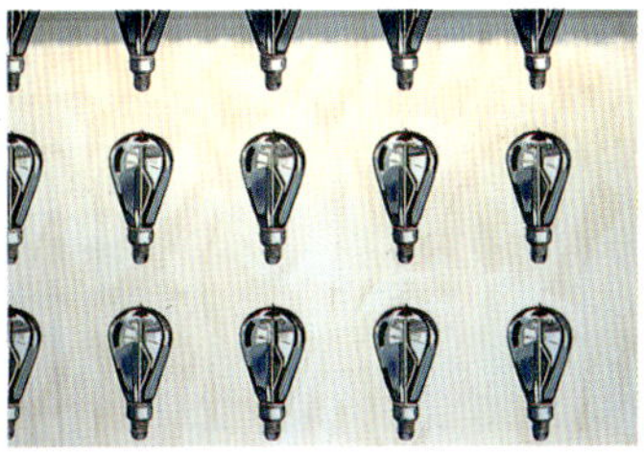

THE TARNISHED ANGELS

Originally created for the Paris Opera Ballet
Paris Opera Ballet Premiere : May 29, 1987 L'Opera de Paris, Paris, France
Armitage Ballet Premiere : September 10, 1987 Doolittle Theater, Los Angeles, California

Choreography : Karole Armitage
Scenery : David Salle
Costumes : Christian Lacroix
Lighting : Ken Tabachnick

Music : The Black Saint and the Sinner Lady.....Charles Mingus

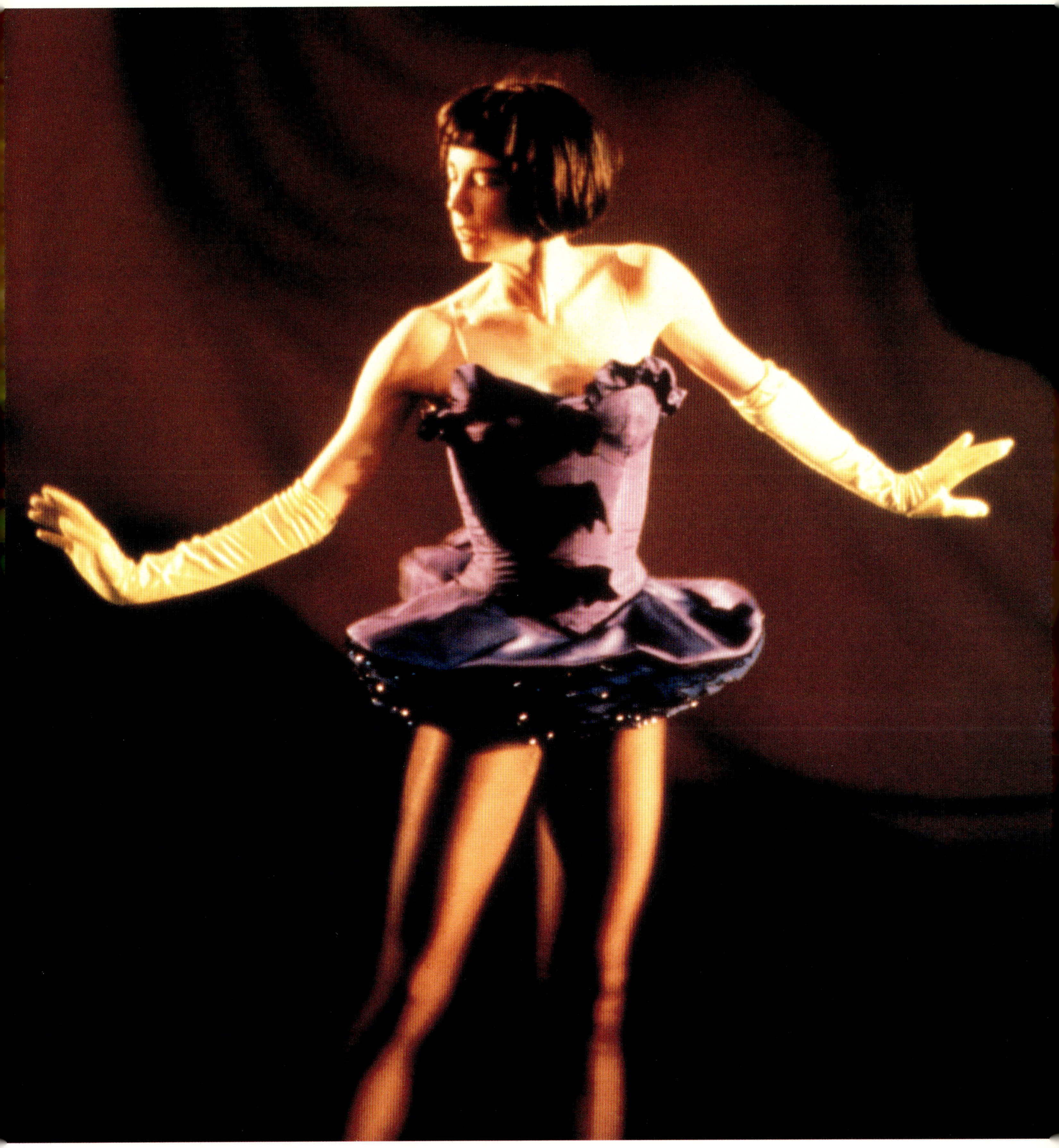

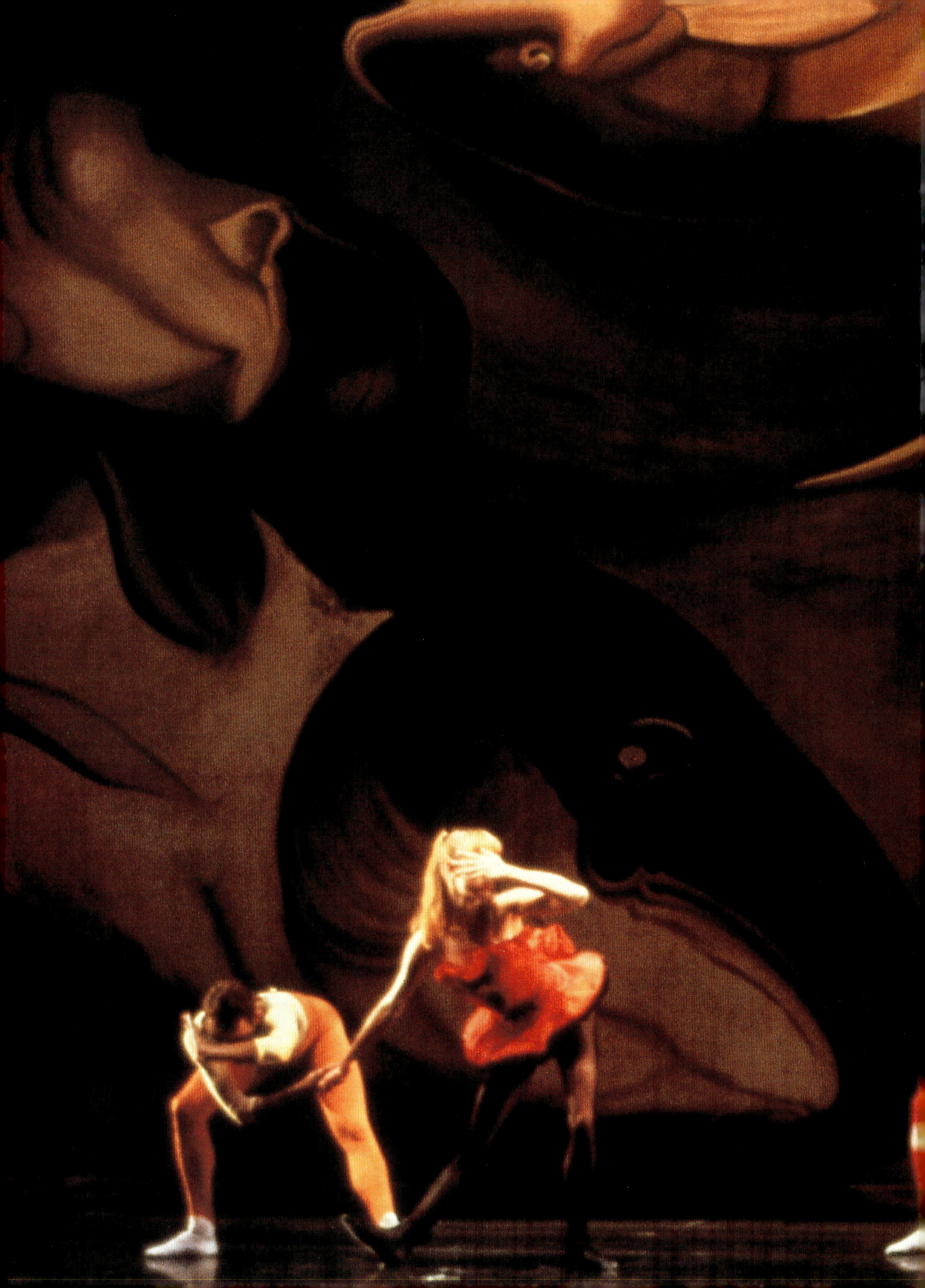

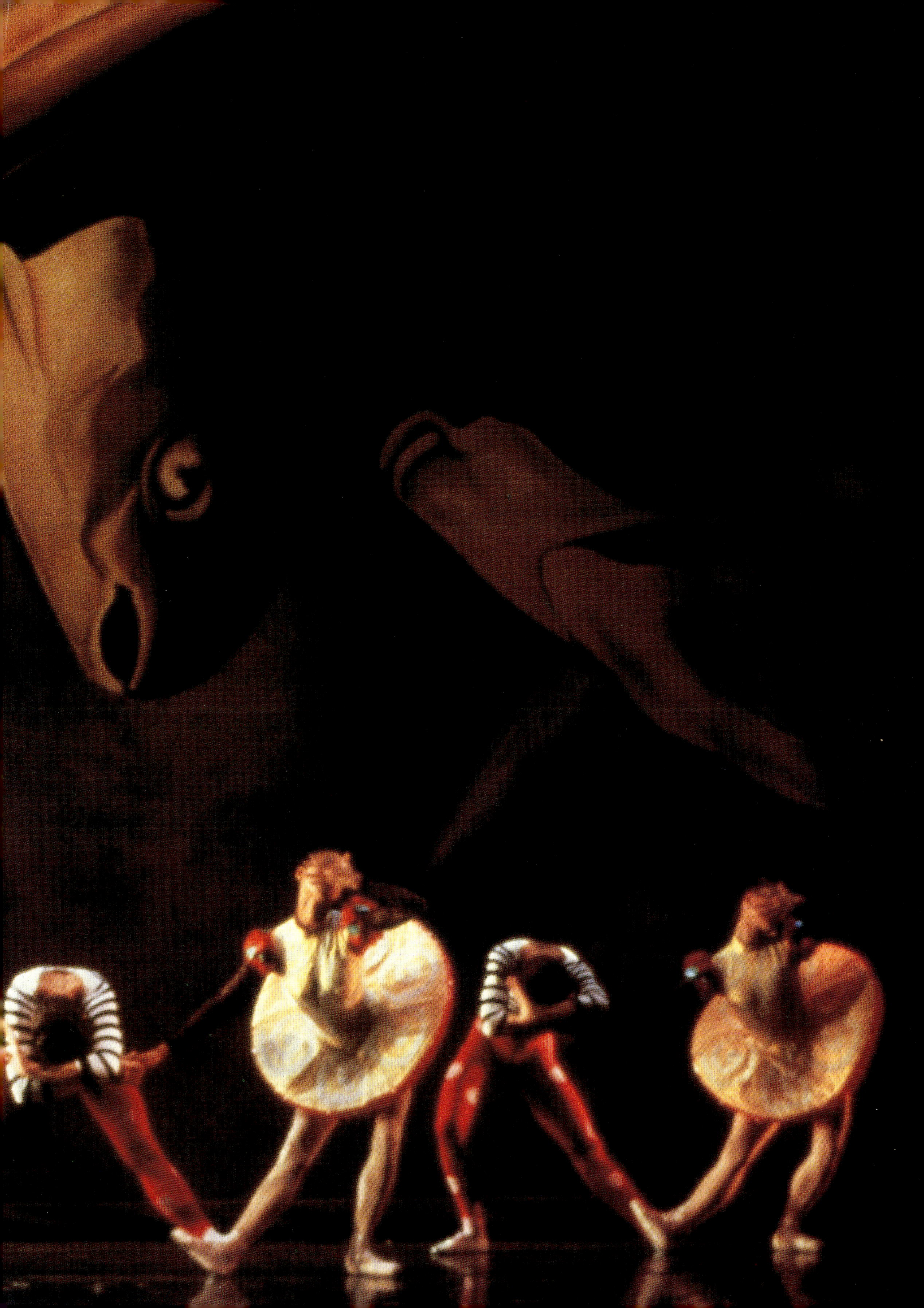

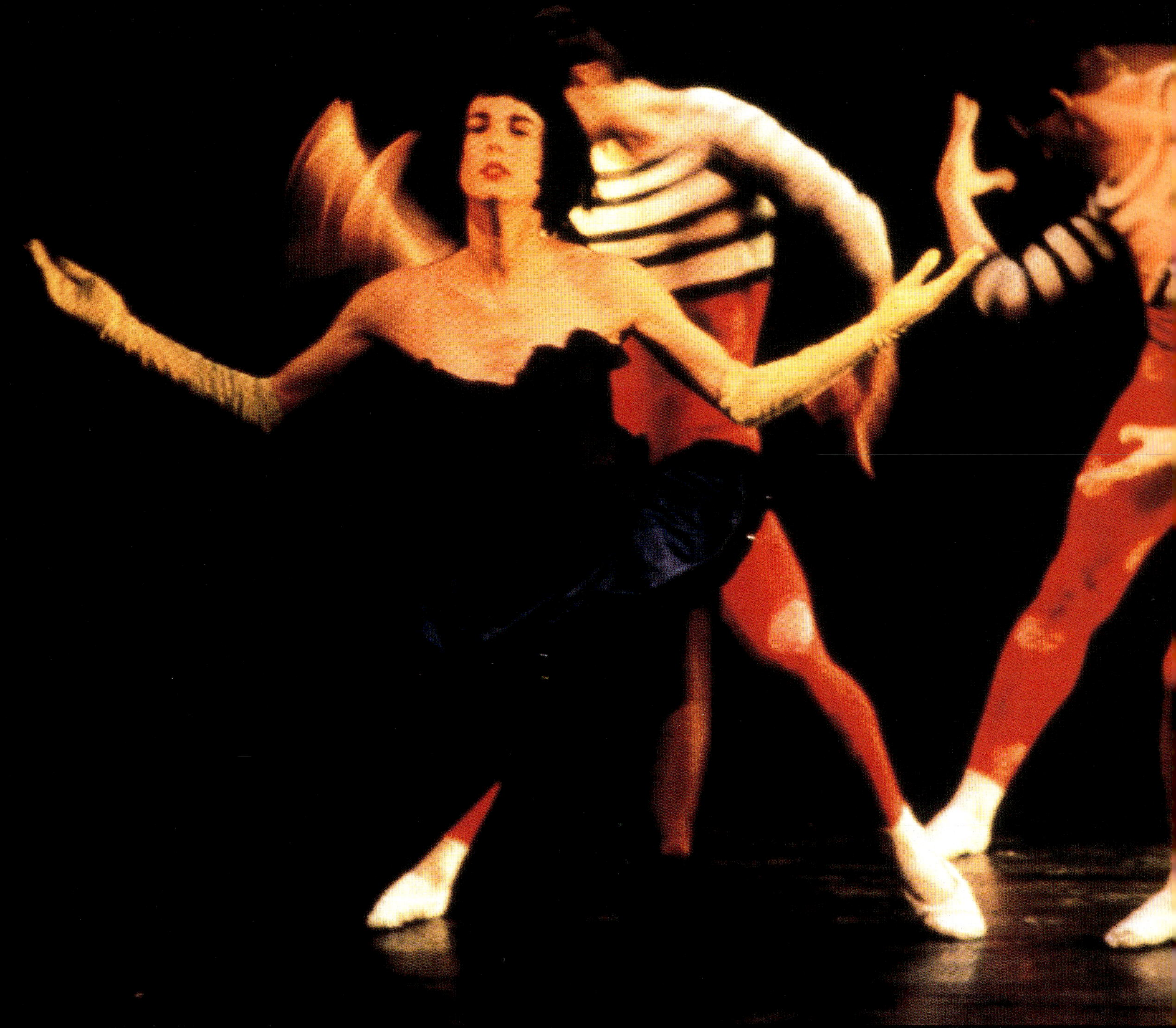
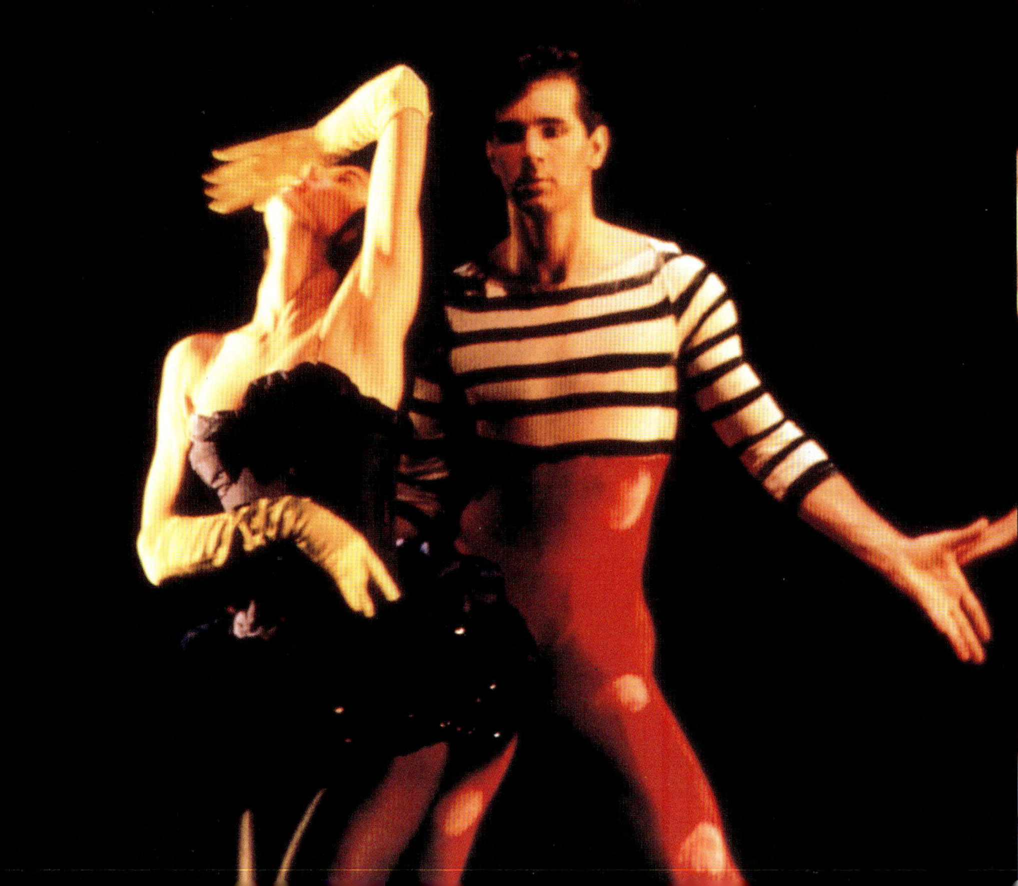
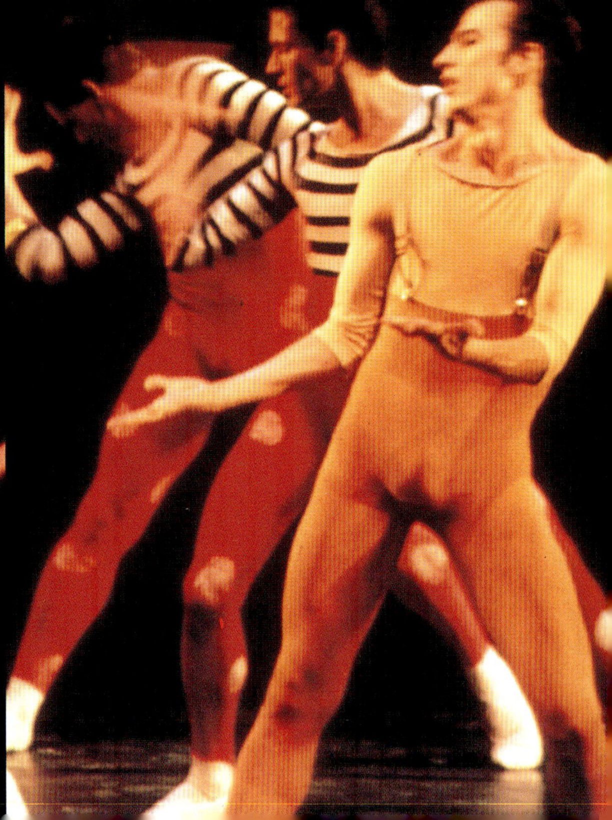

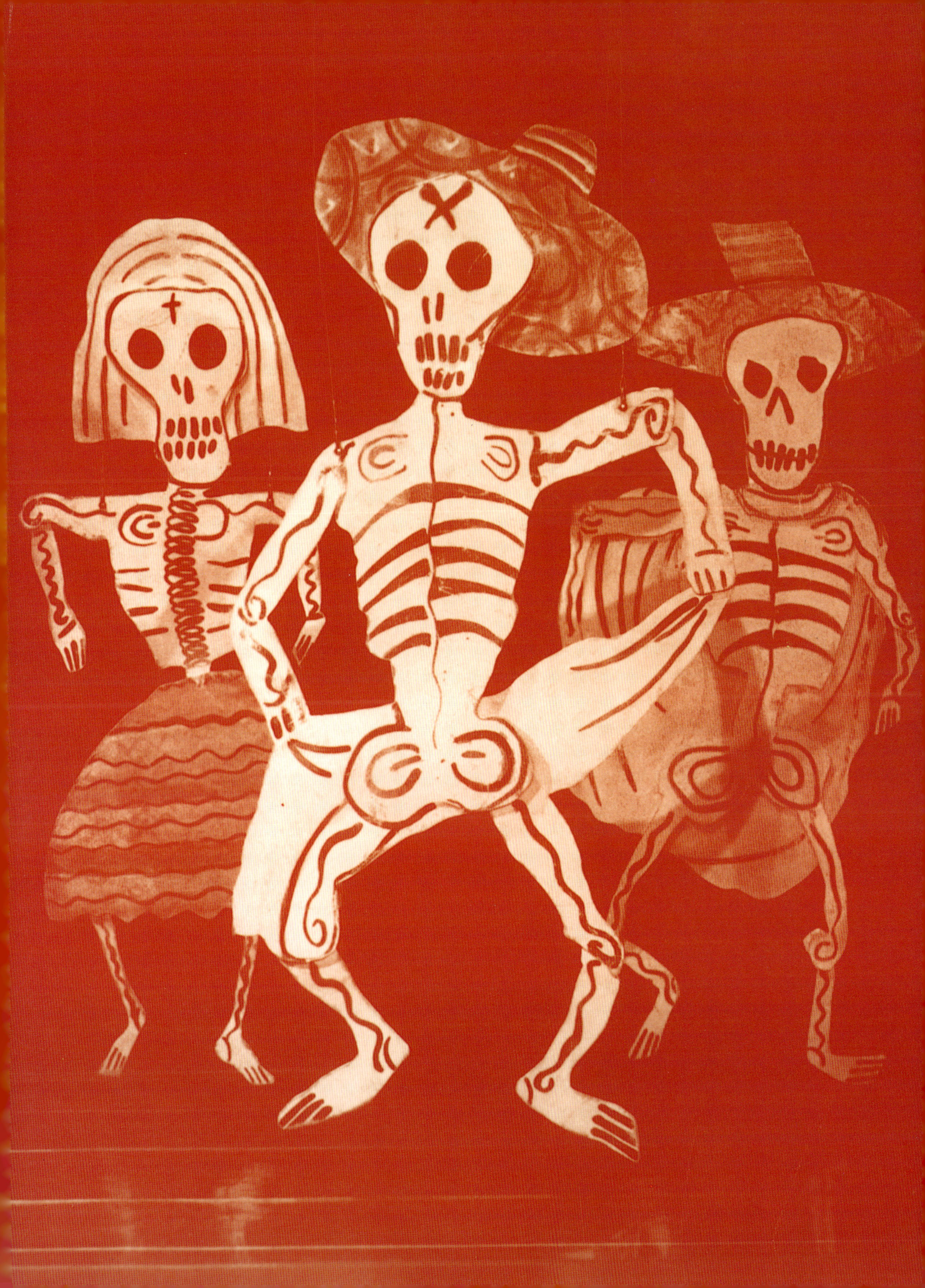

KAMMERDISCO

Armitage Ballet Premiere: April 10, 1988. Sao Paulo, Brazil

Choreography : Karole Armitage
Costumes and Scenery : David Salle
Lighting : Debra Dumas
Music : Jeffrey Lohn

DUCK DANCES

Premiere : April 30, 1988, Angers, France

Choreography : Karole Armitage
Costumes : David Salle
Lighting : Debra Dumas

Music

Duck Dance..Jeffrey Lohn

Crucifixus..J.S. Bach
arranged by Jeffrey Lohn

Oh My God...Jeffrey Lohn

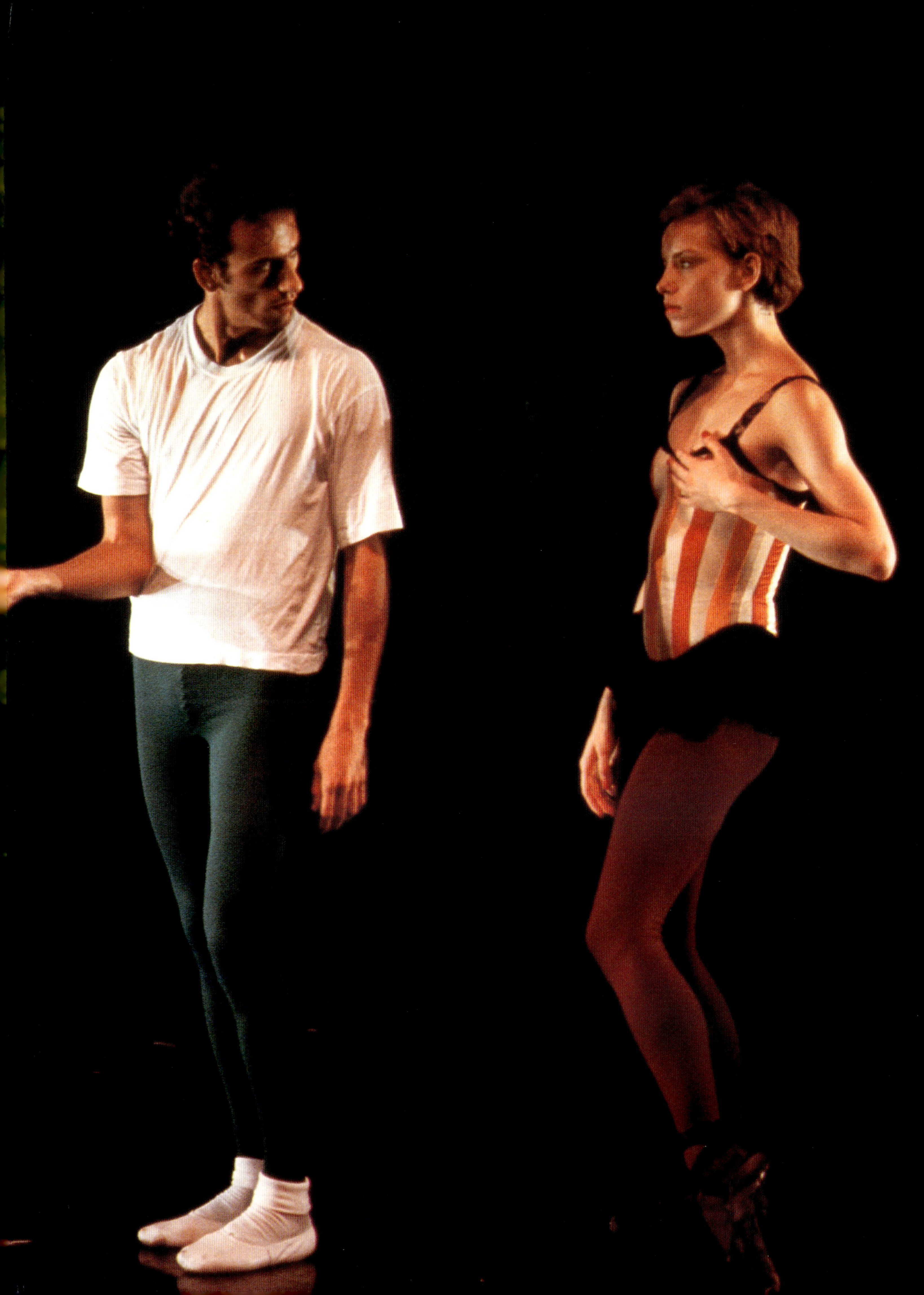

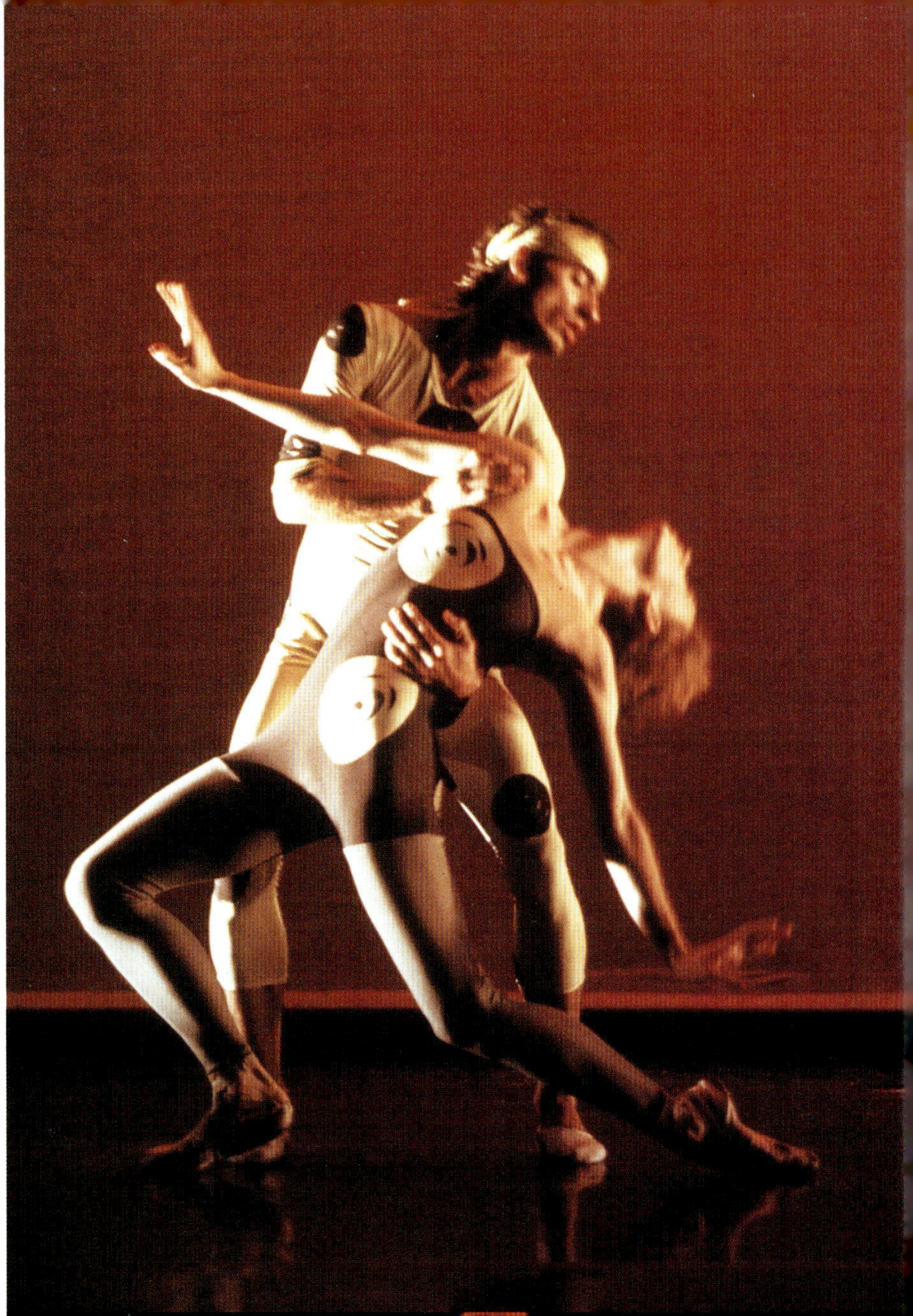
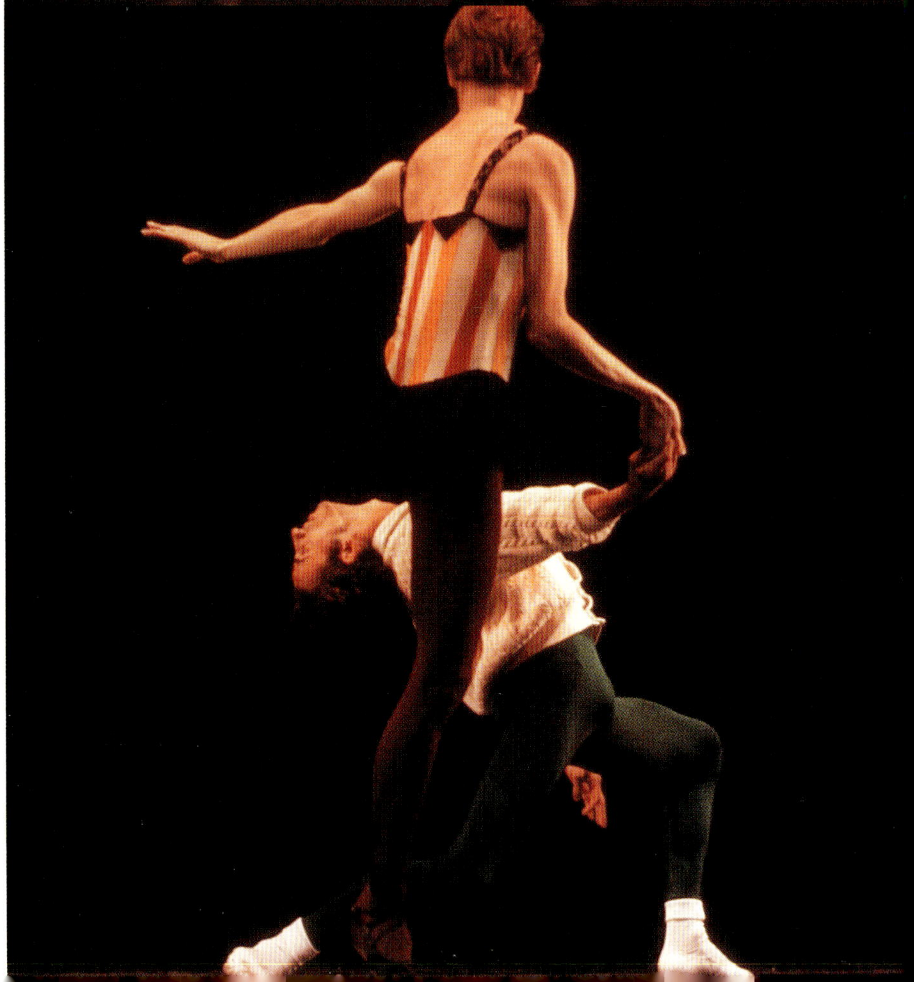

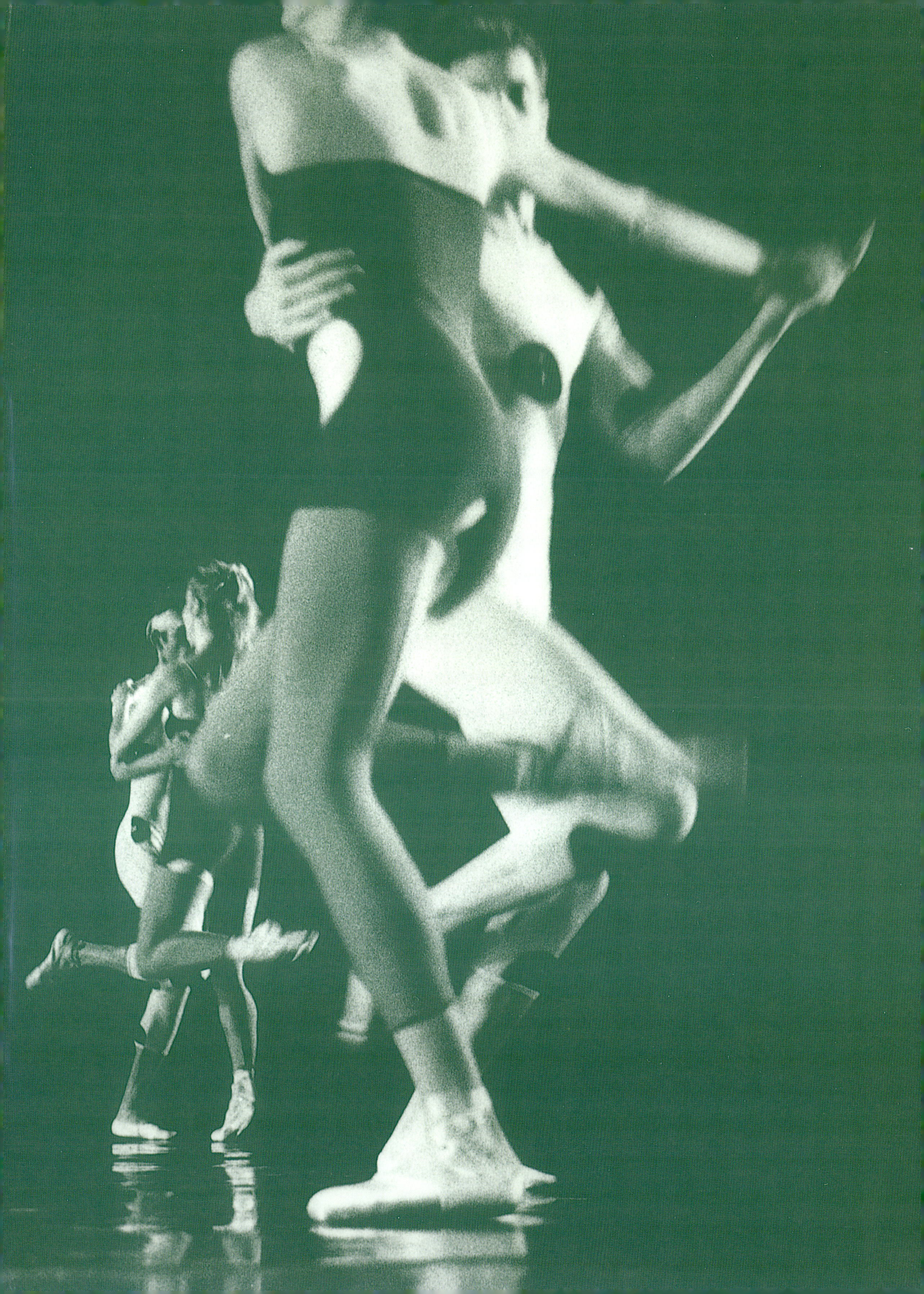

GO GO BALLERINA

Armitage Ballet Premiere: November 13, 1988
The World, New York, New York

Choreography : Karole Armitage
Scenery : Jeff Koons
Costumes : David Salle and Jeff Koons
Lighting : Ken Tabachnick

Music

Manic Depression........................ Jimi Hendrix

Show Em Wacha Got........................ Public Enemy

Rebel Without a Pause..................... Public Enemy

Mr. Big Dick.................................... Schooly D.

Suck'n' Swallow................................ The Hard-Ons

Wild Thing....................................... Jimi Hendrix

Fire.. Jimi Hendrix

I Don't Live Today............................ Jimi Hendrix

Hey Joe.. Jimi Hendrix

All Along the Watchtower................ Jimi Hendrix

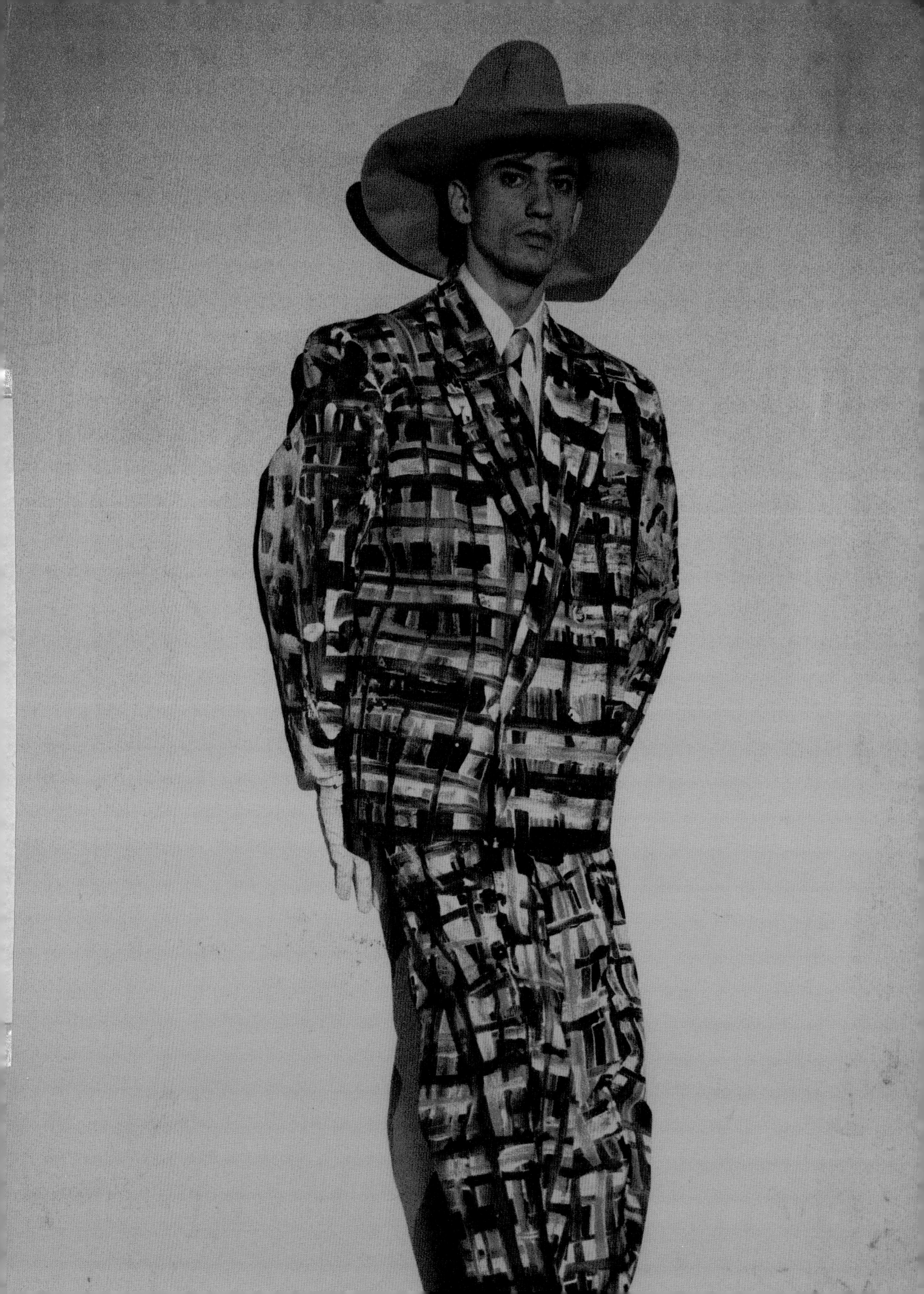

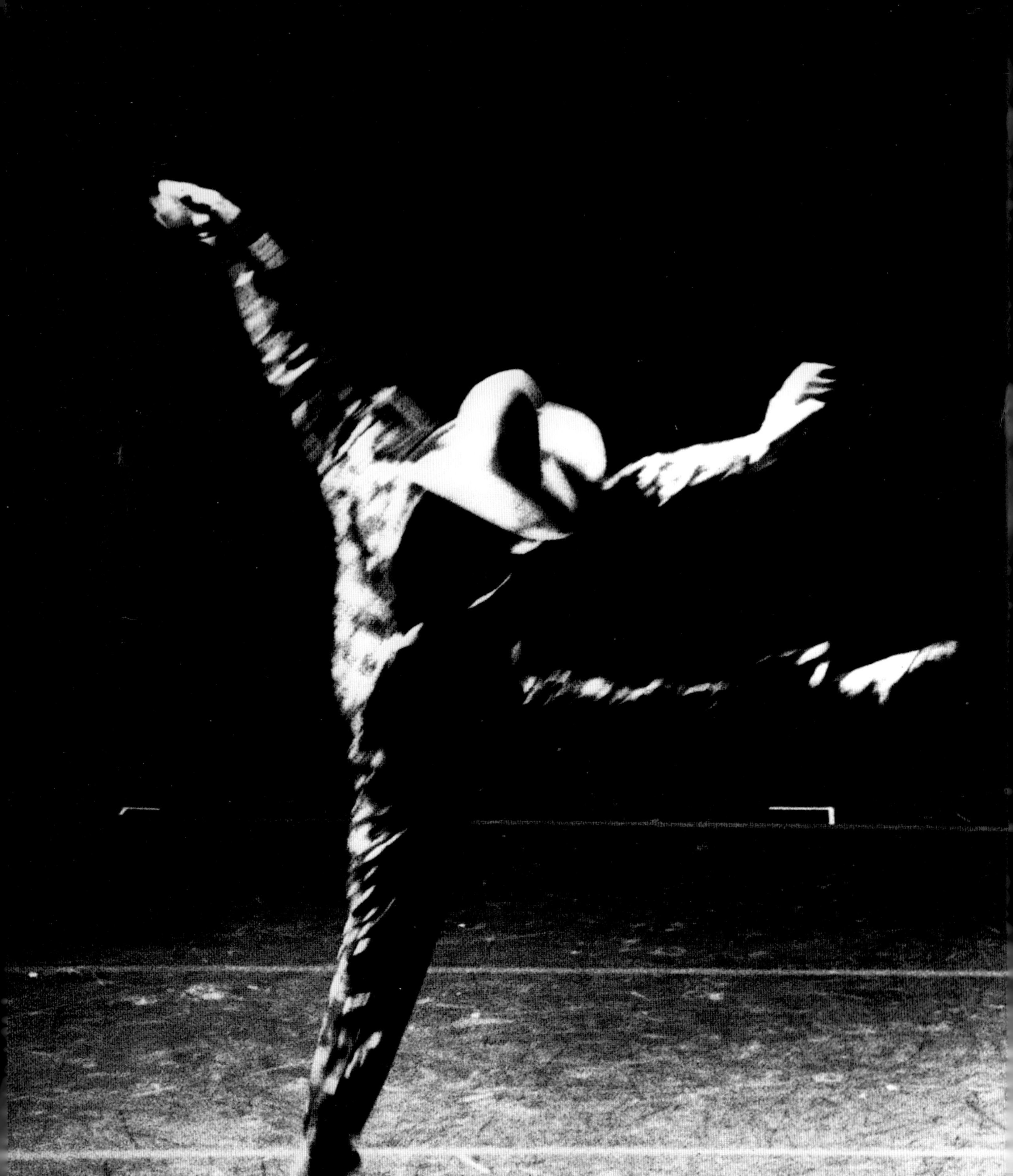

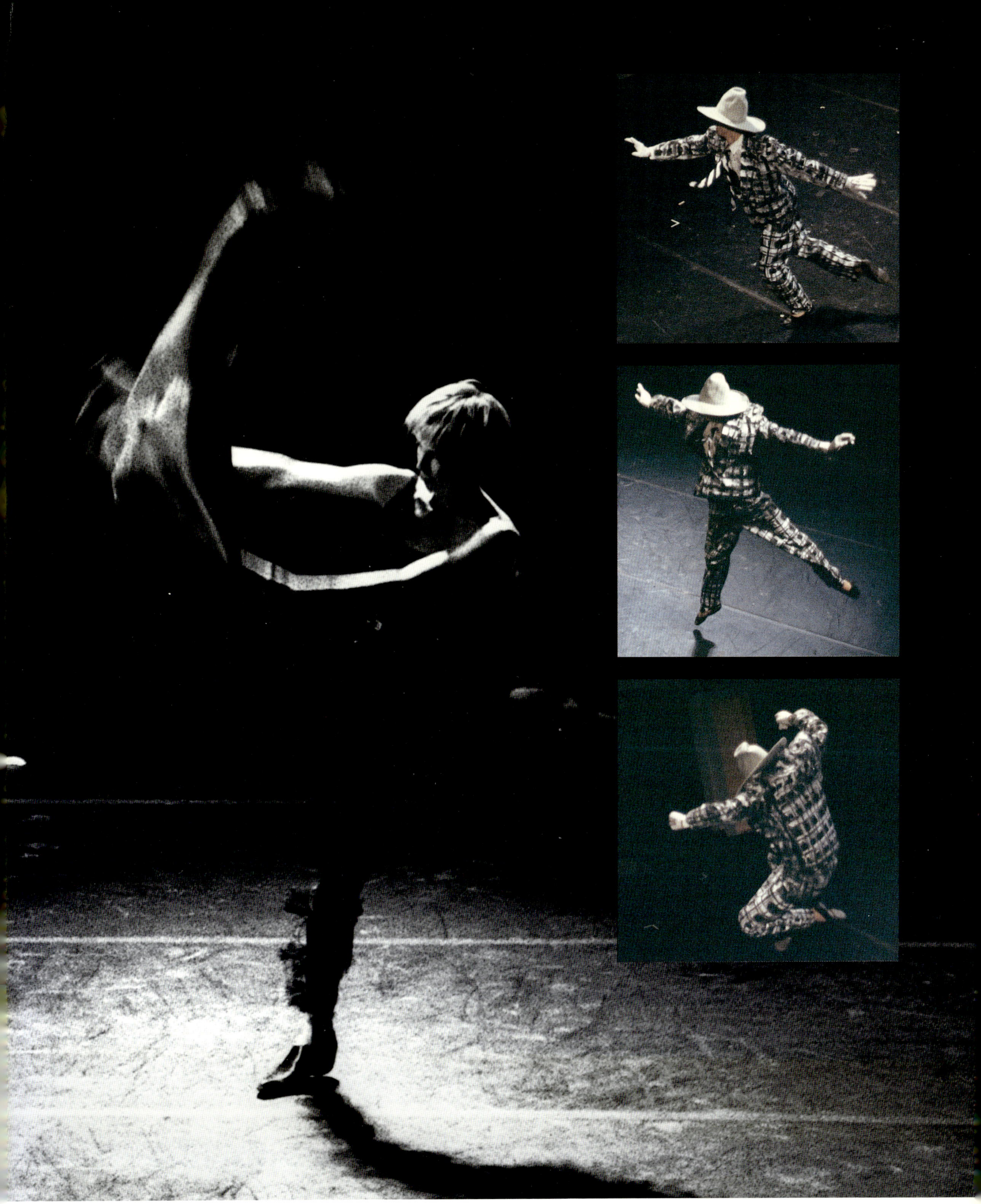

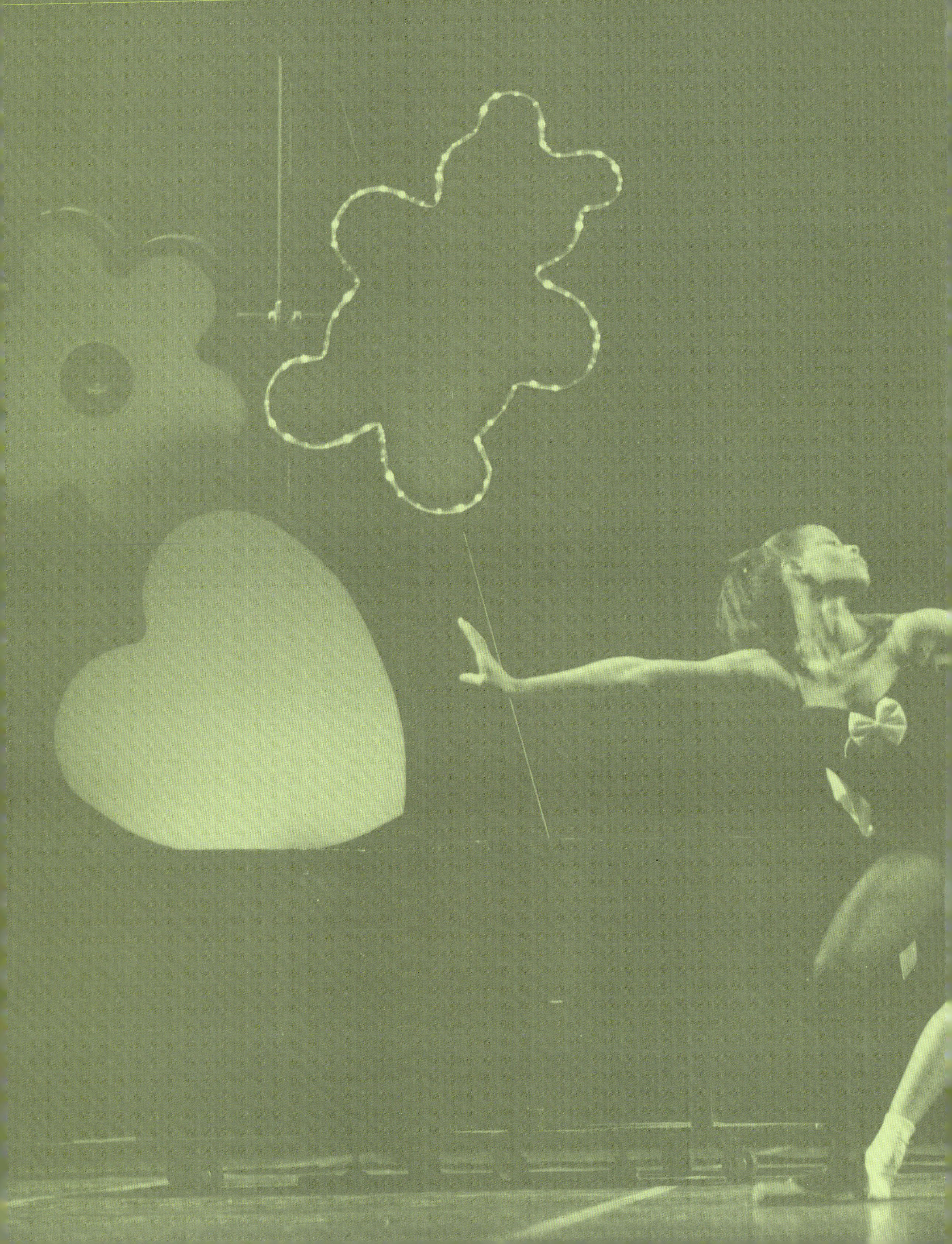

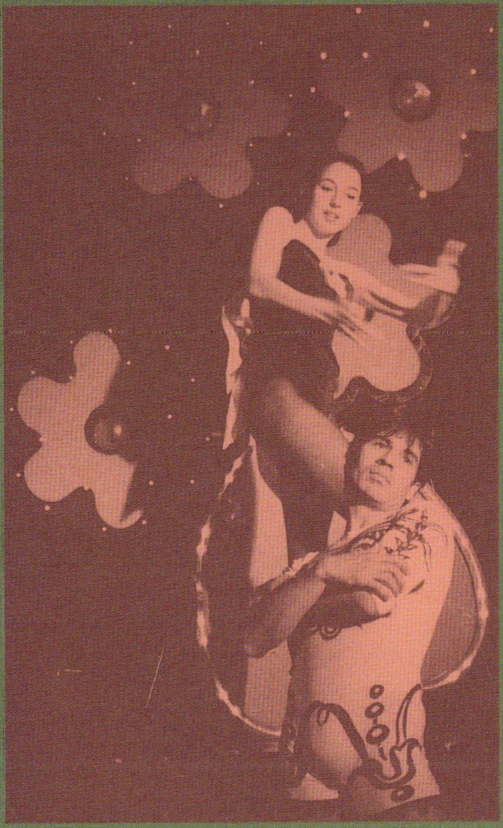
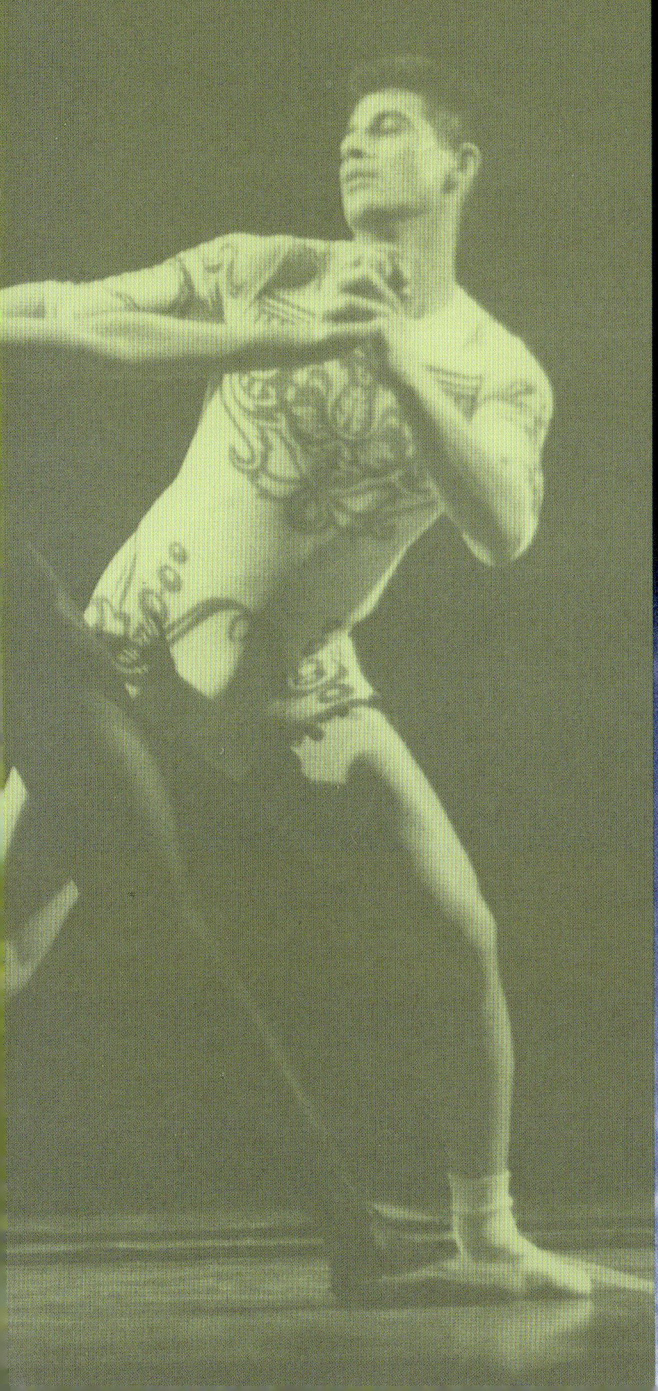
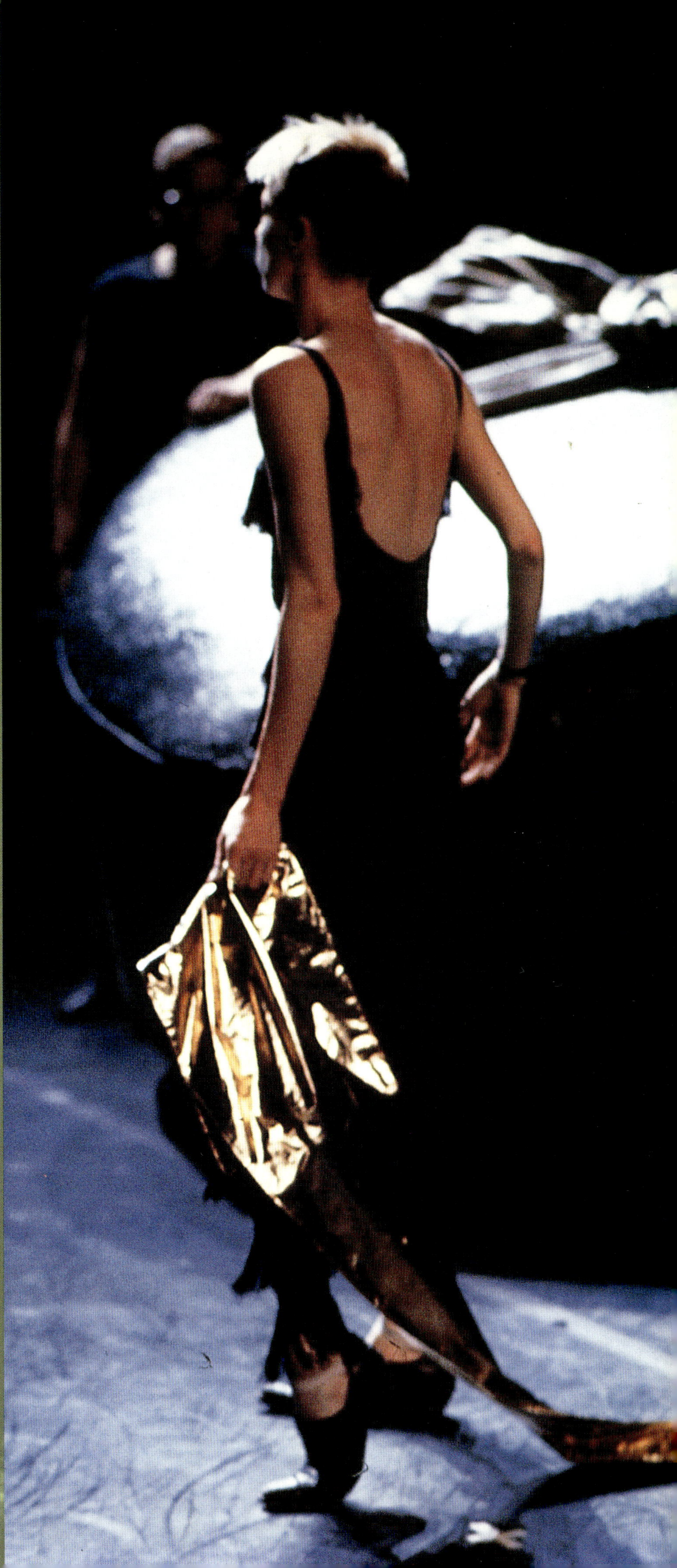

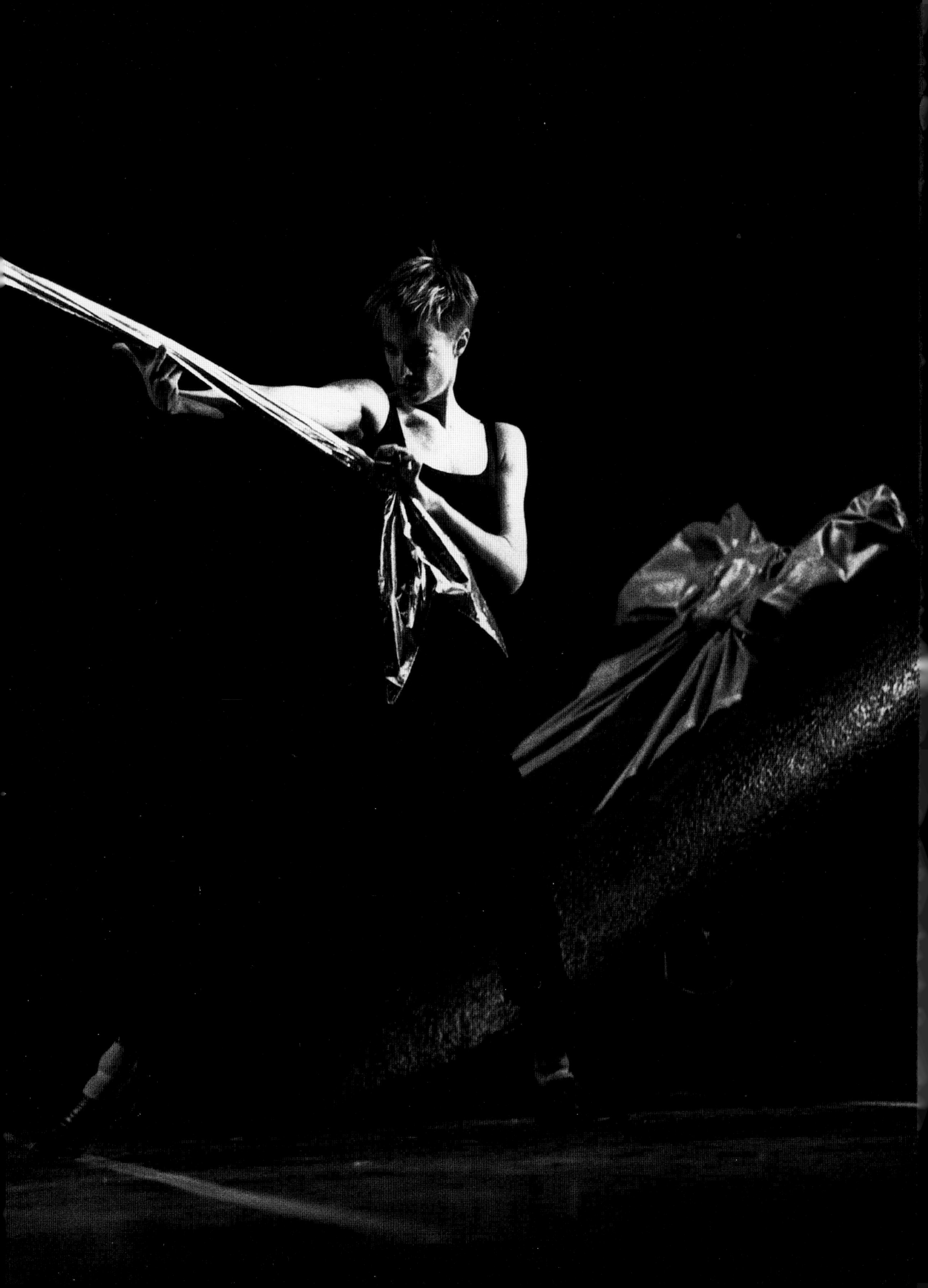

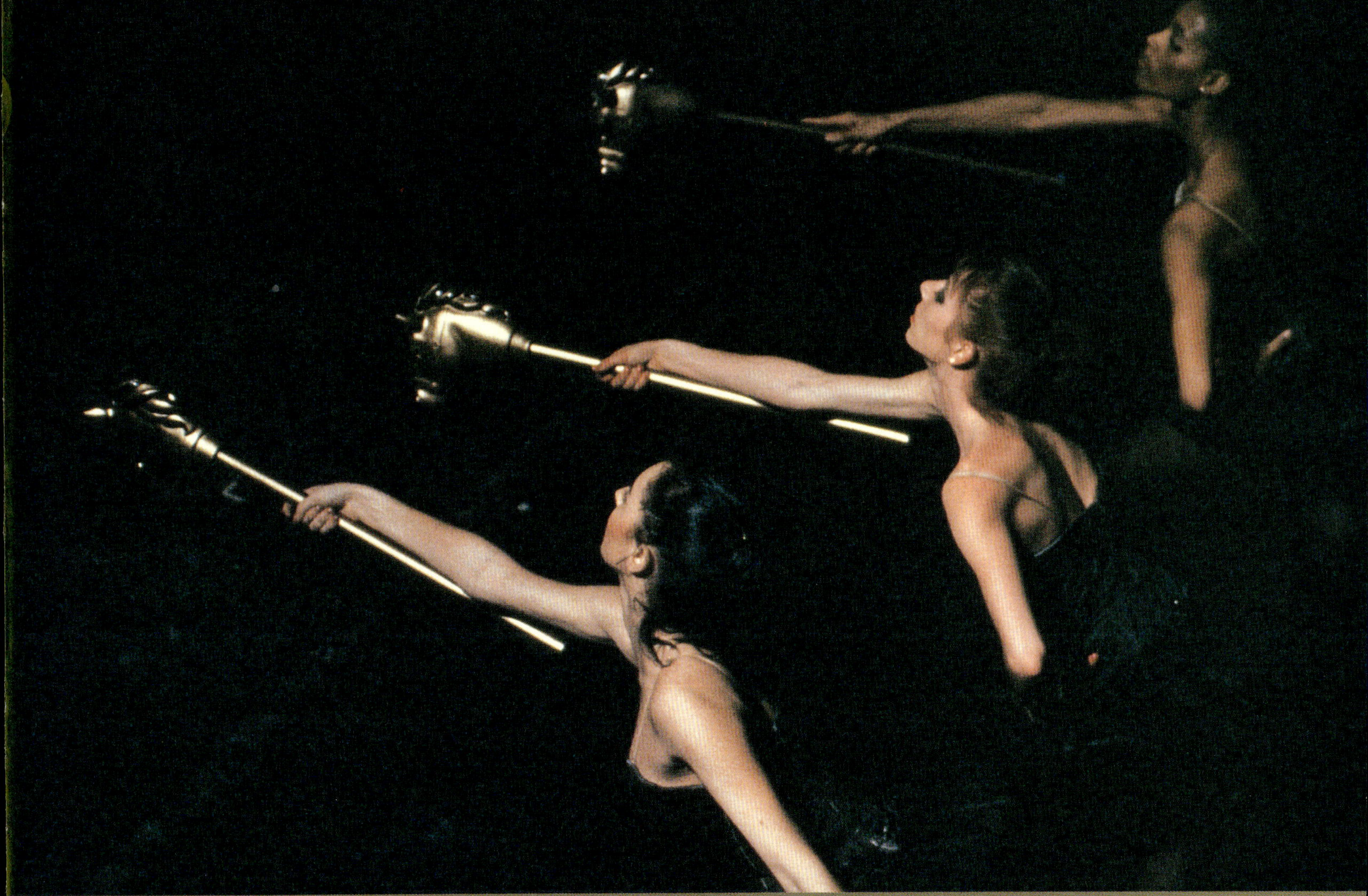

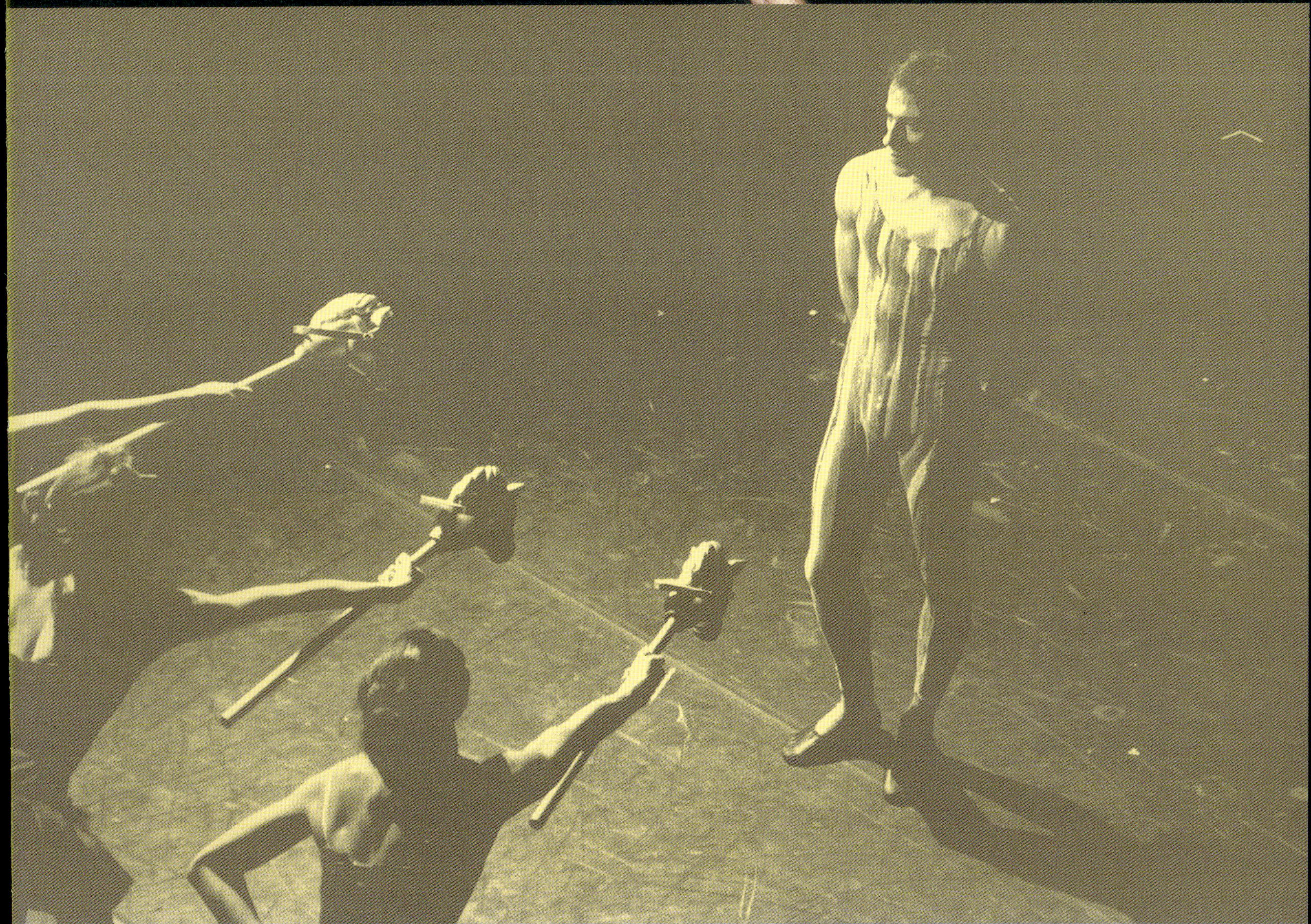

CONTEMPT

The Armitage Ballet Premiere : April 11, 1989,
Le Quartz, Brest, France

Choreography : Karole Armitage
Scenery and Costumes : David Salle and Jeff Koons
Lighting : Ken Tabachnick
Inflatable Pig Sculpture : Ann Slavit

Music

I. Prelude:

The Gangster and His Moll
Brilliant Corners.. Thelonious Monk

The Boxer and His Wife (Mike Tyson and Robin Givens)
Blue Bolivar Ba-lues-are........................... Thelonious Monk

The Painter and His Model
Crepuscule with Nellie.............................. Thelonious Monk

The Photographer and His Model
Switch Blade... Duke Ellington/Charles Mingus

II. My Funny Valentine.........................Rodgers & Hart, sung by Chet Baker

III. Money Jungle...................................Duke Ellington

IV. Why do I sleep with Franklin?......... Bret Easton Ellis

V. African Flower.................................Duke Ellington

VI. Hog Callin' Blues.............................. Charles Mingus

VII. Bilbao Song..................................... Kurt Weill
arranged by Gil Evans

VIII. Sarabande in D Minor.......................J.S. Bach

IX. Excerpts from Spillane.....................John Zorn

X. "Elegy" from String Quartet #15.......Dimitri Shostakovich

XI. The Thrill is Gone............................ Chet Baker

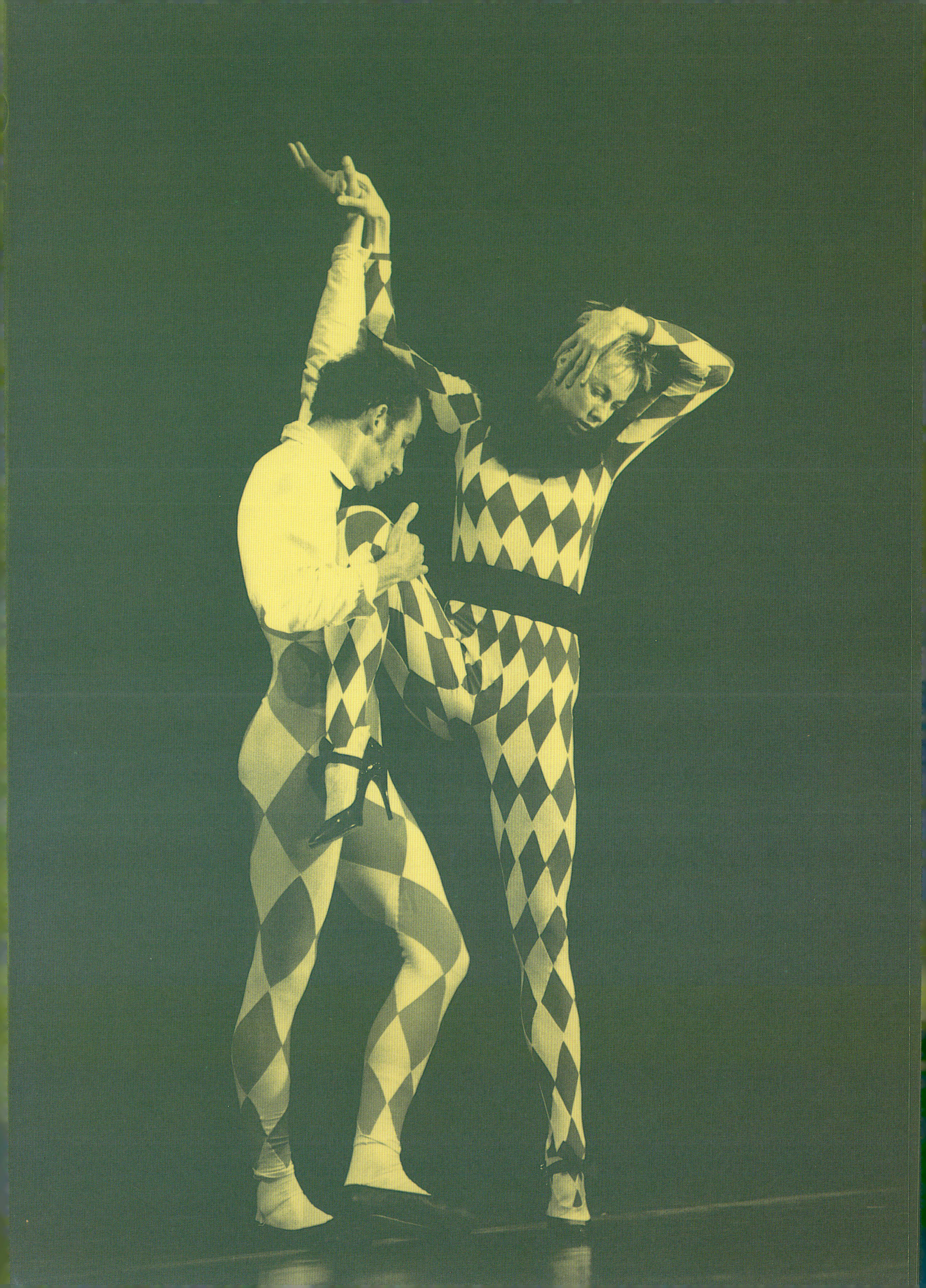

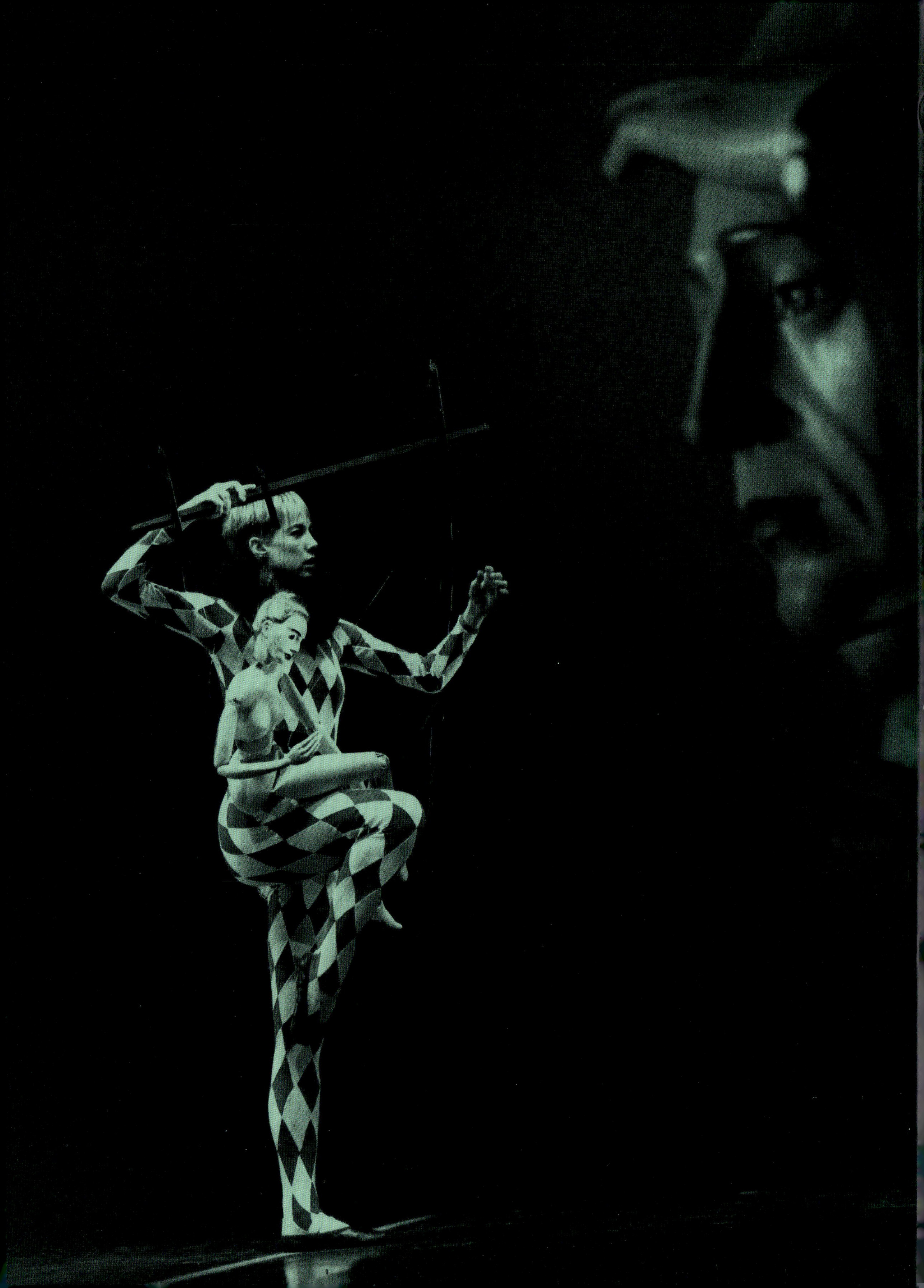

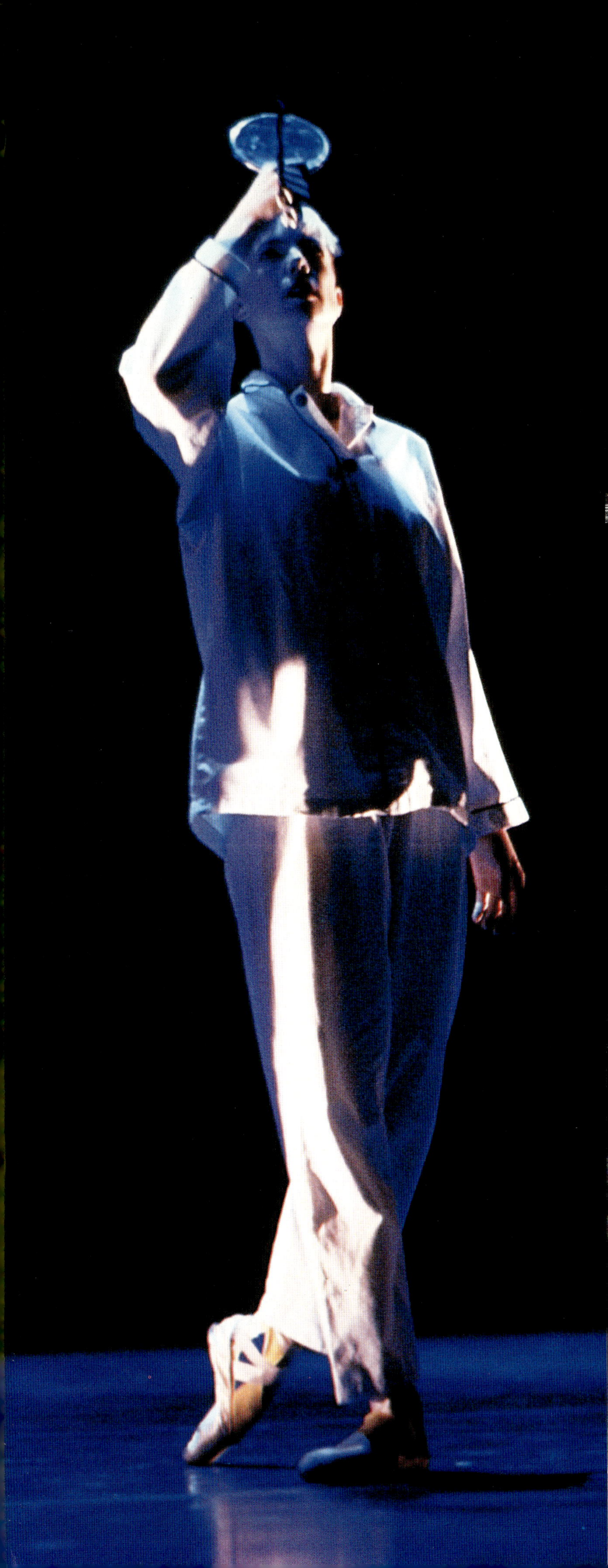
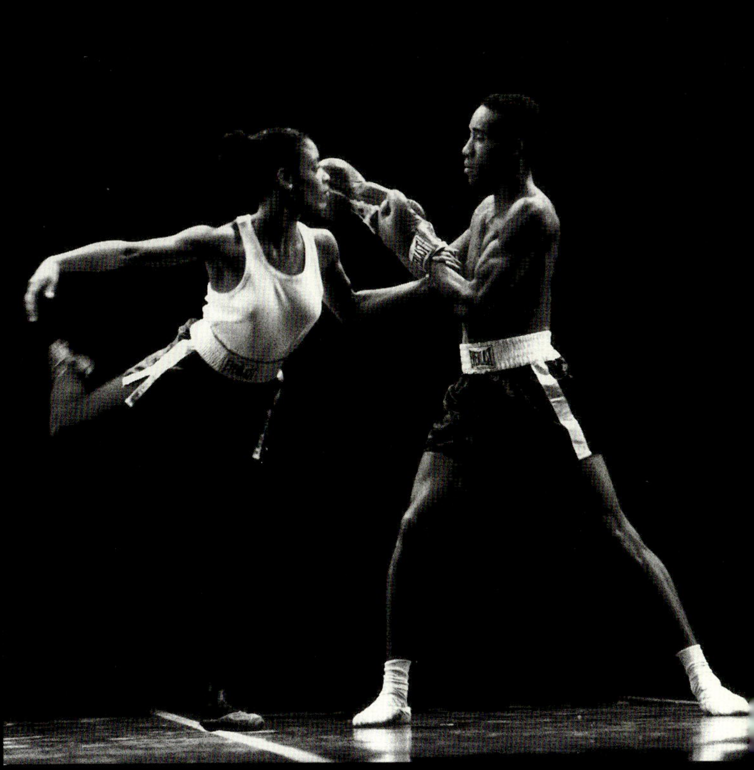
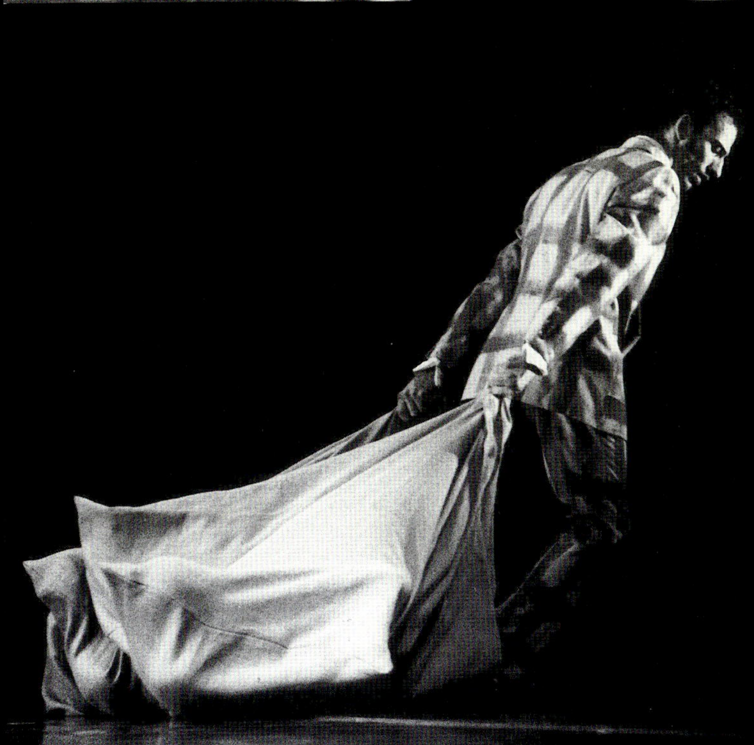
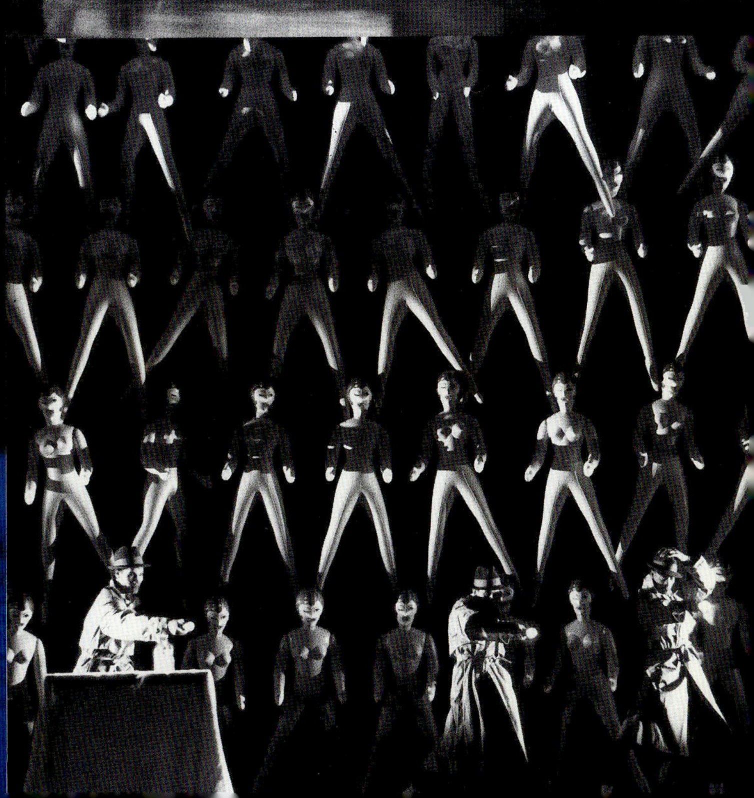

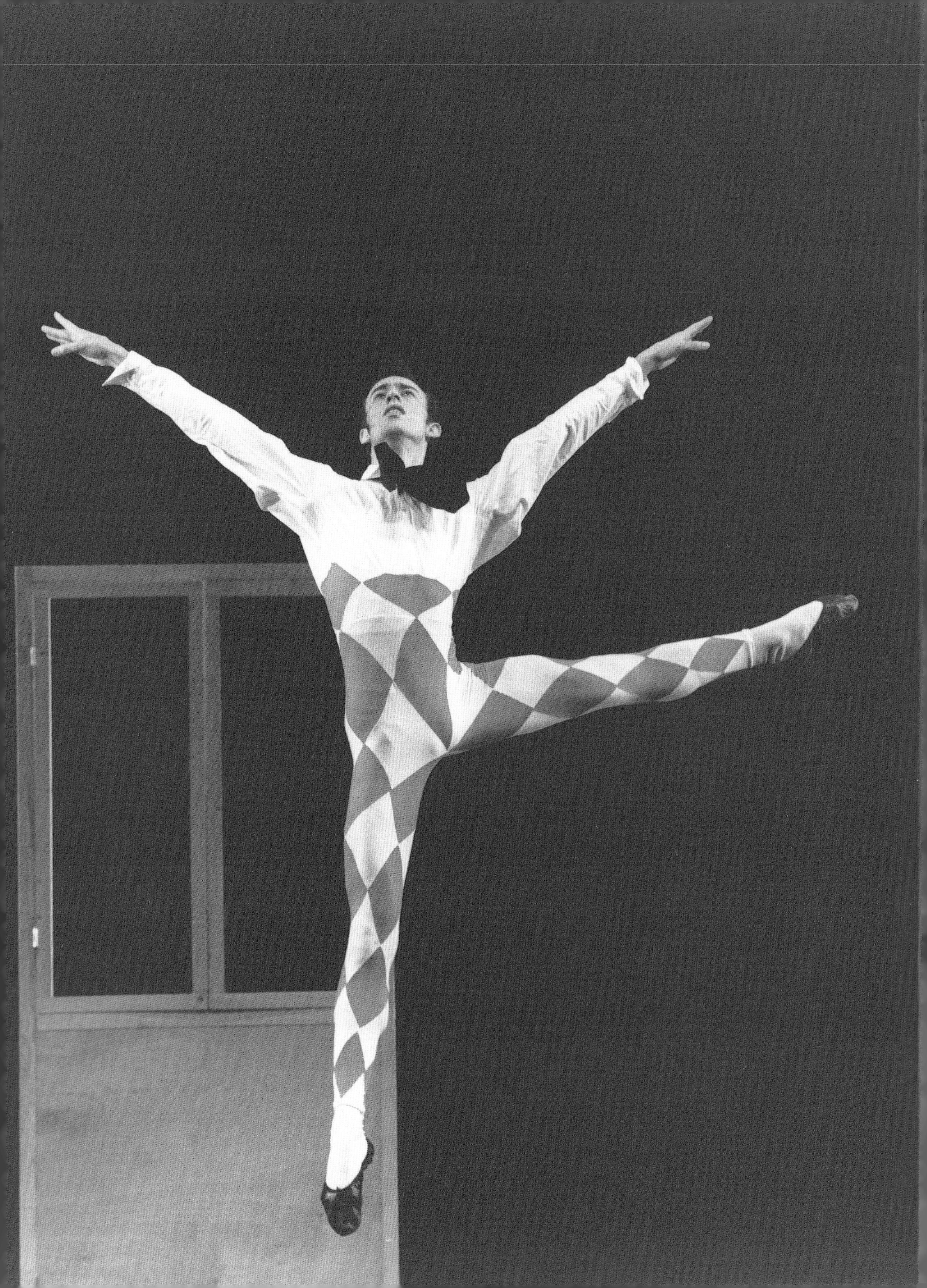

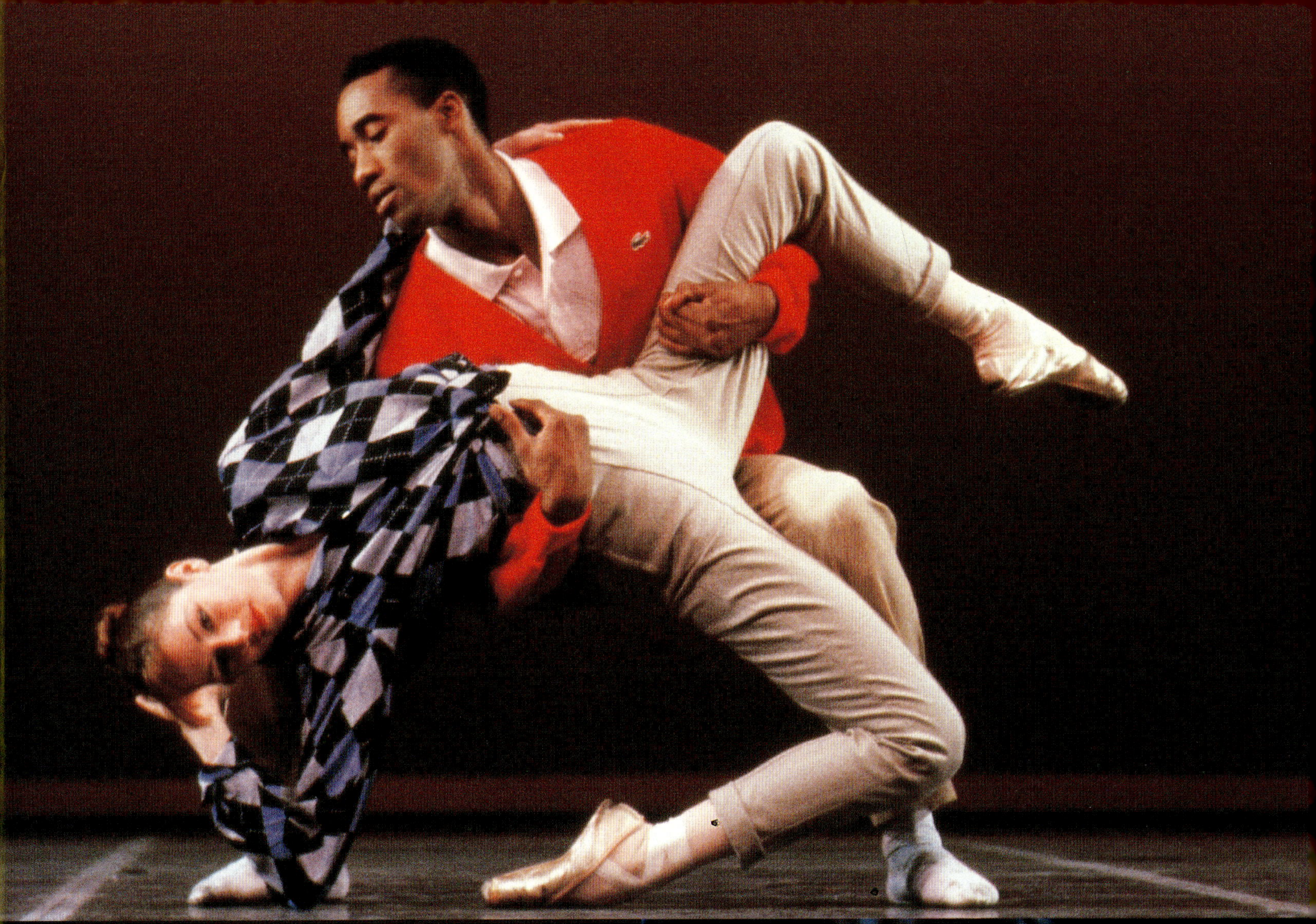
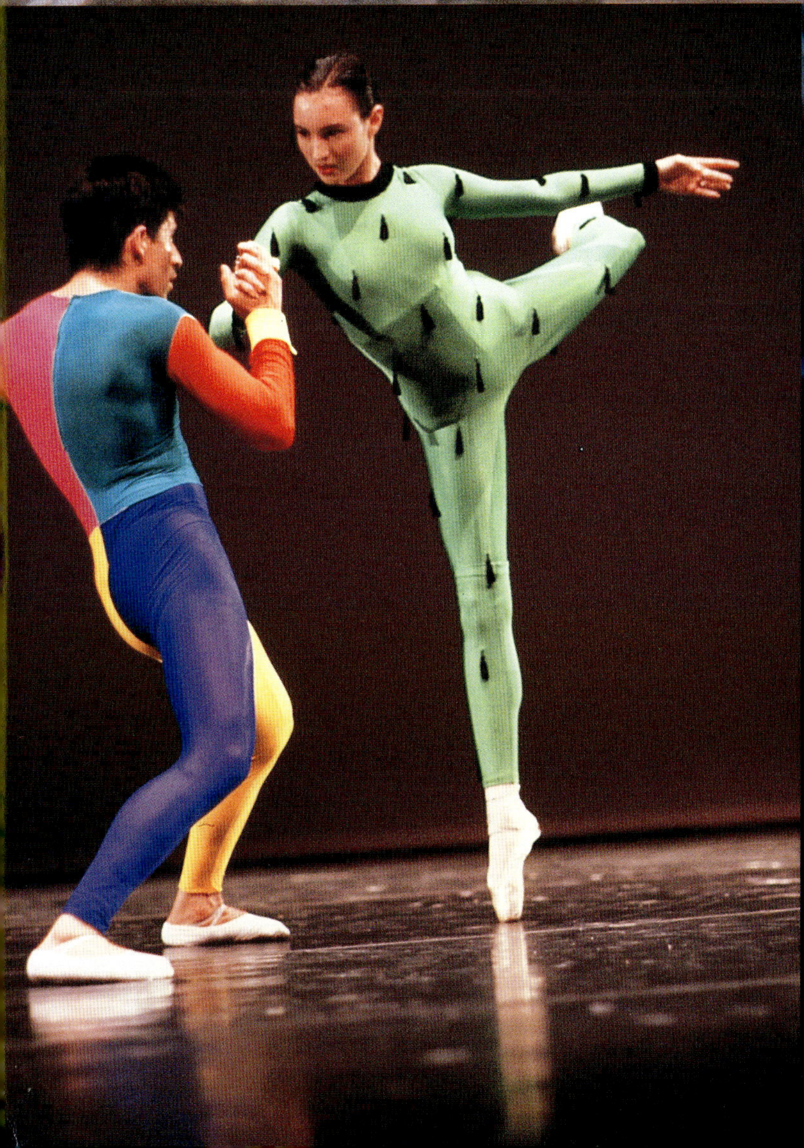
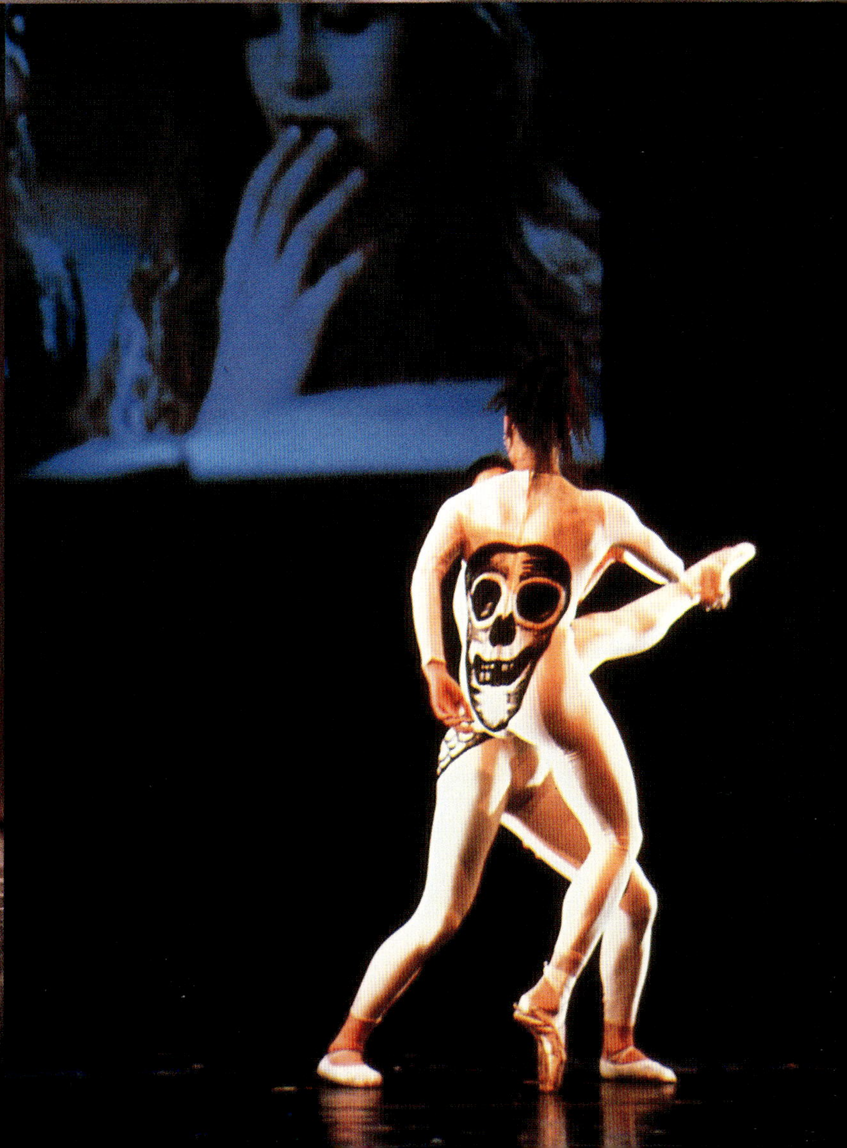

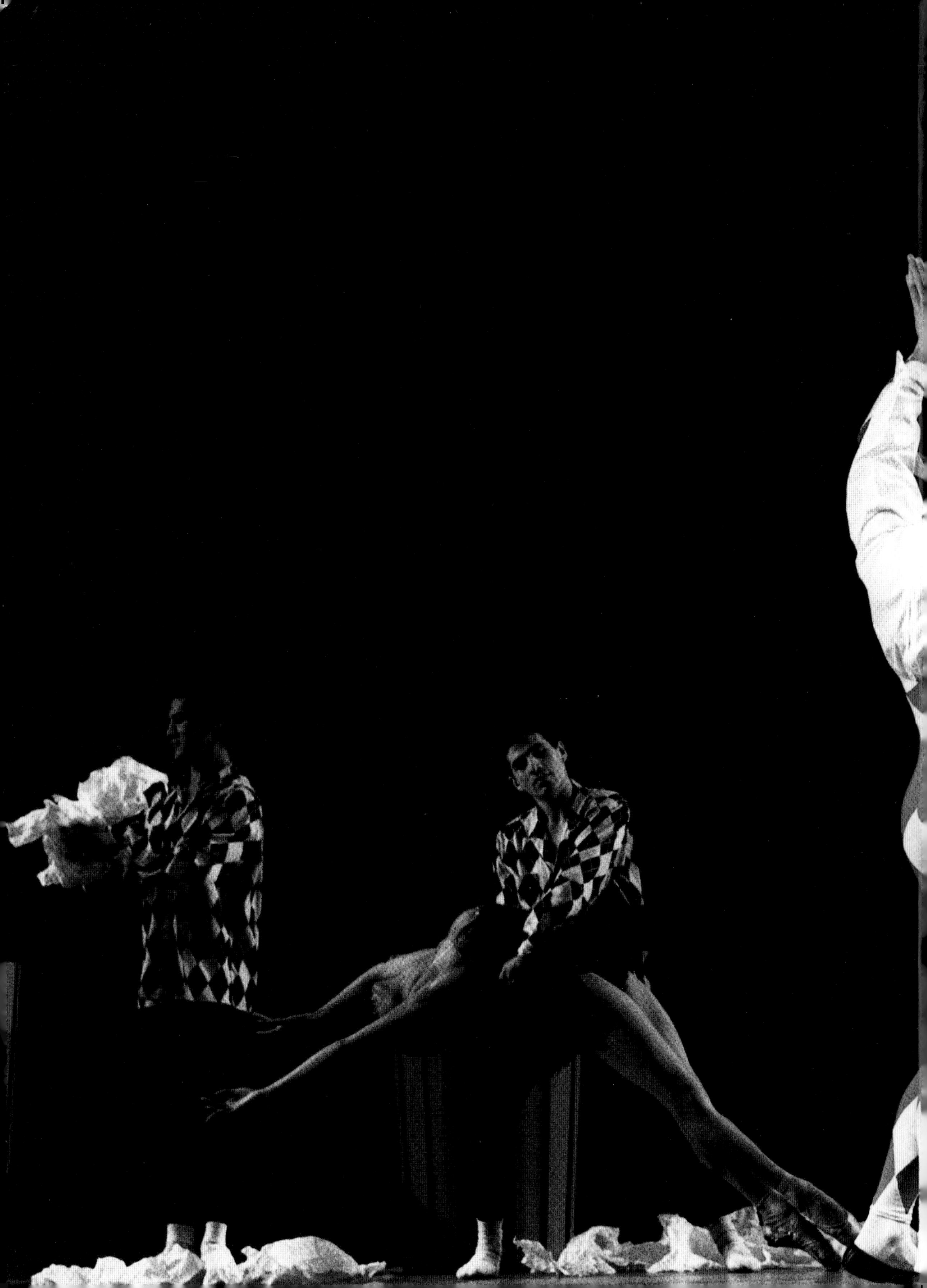

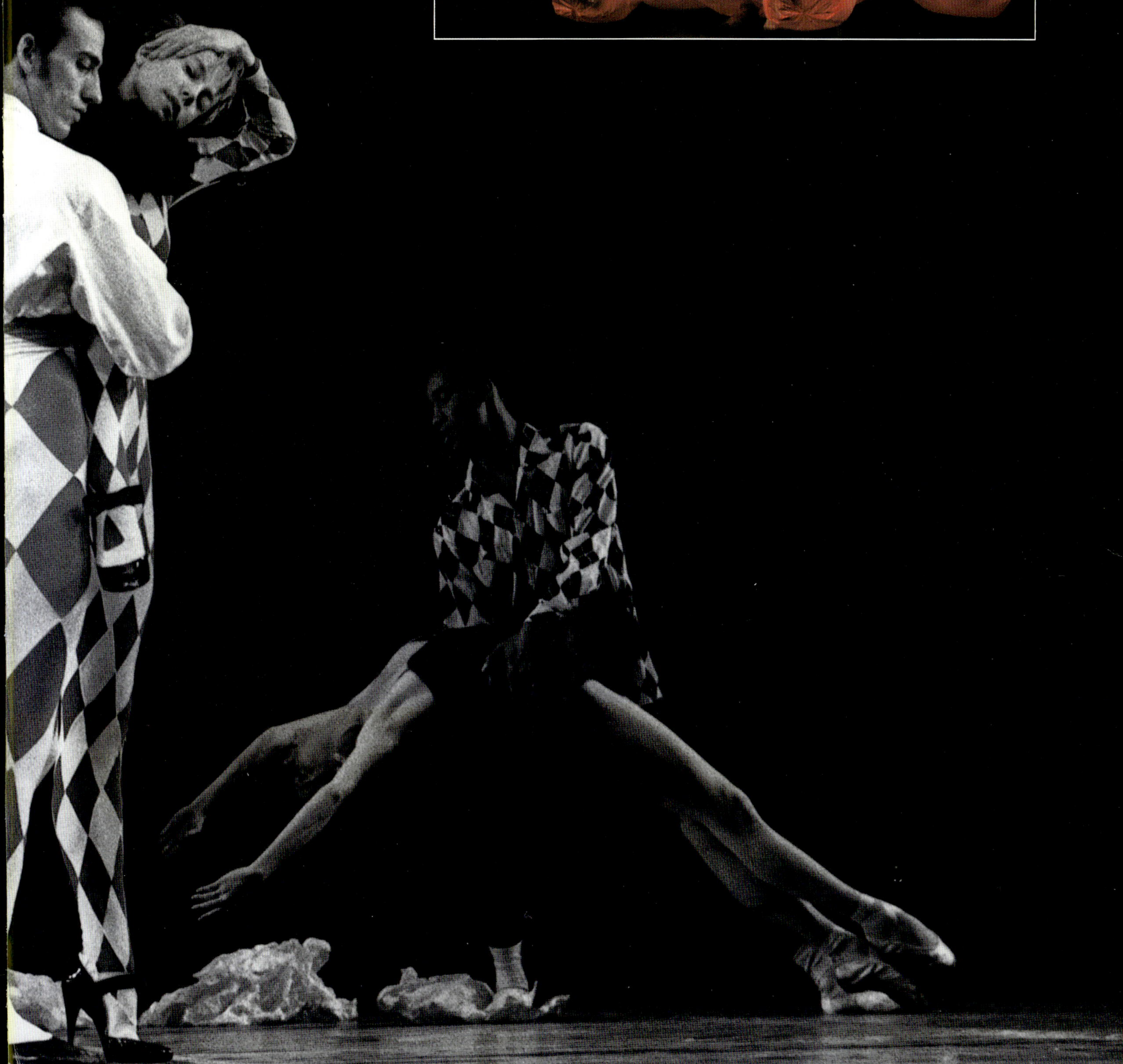
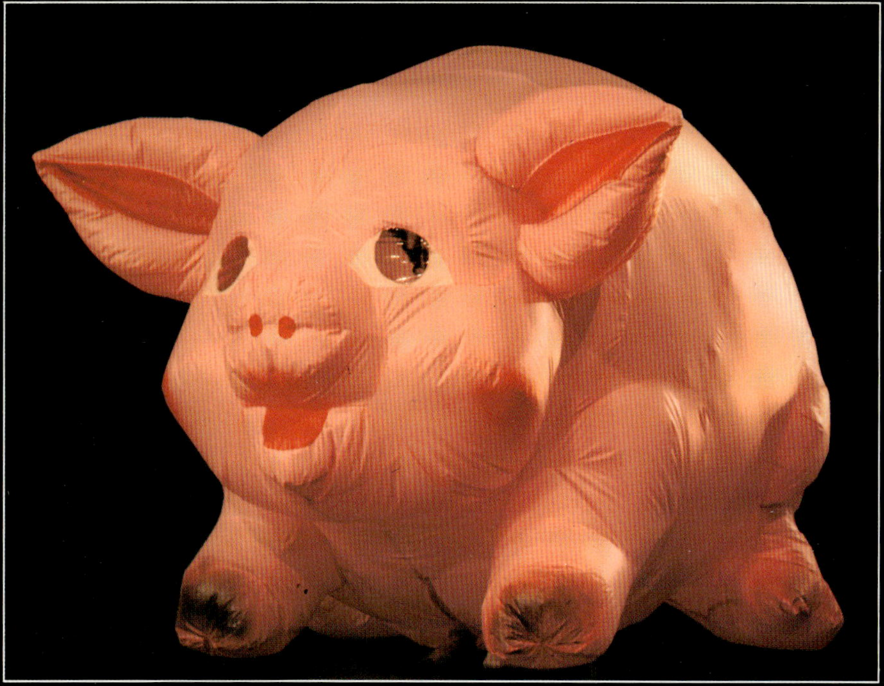

PHOTO CREDITS

PAGE#	PHOTOGRAPHER
cover photo	Gianfranco Gorgoni
page 7	Richard N. Greenhouse
page 8	Richard N. Greenhouse
	Martha Swope
page 9	Martha Swope
page 10	Martha Swope
page 11	Martha Swope
	Martha Swope
page 13	Julio Donoso
page 14	Monroe Warshaw
page 15	Gianfranco Gorgoni
page 16	Monroe Warshaw
page 17	Gianfranco Gorgoni
page 18	Monroe Warshaw
	Monroe Warshaw
	Anne Nordmann
	Colette Masson
page 19	Gianfranco Gorgoni
	Gianfranco Gorgoni
	Gianfranco Gorgoni
page 20-21	Julio Donoso
page 21	Jacques Hoepffner
page 21	Jacques Hoepffner
page 21	Jacques Hoepffner
page 21	Jacques Heopffner
page 21	Jacques Hoepffner
page 21	Jacques Hoepffner
page 21	Jacques Hoepffner
page 23	Michi Imai
page 24-25	Gianfranco Gorgoni
page 26	Michi Imai
	Michael Moran
page 27	Monroe Warshaw
page 29	Richard Bowditch
page 30	Richard Bowditch
	Gianfranco Gorgoni
	Richard Bowditch
	Richard Bowditch
page 31	Monroe Warshaw
page 33	Kent Correll
page 34-35	Kent Correll
page 35	Gianfranco Gorgoni
page 35	Gianfranco Gorgoni
page 35	Gianfranco Gorgoni
page 36-37	Colette Masson
page 37	Tiziano Magni
page 38	Colette Masson
page 39	Gianfranco Gorgoni
	Gianfranco Gorgoni
page 41	Colette Masson
page 42	Colette Masson
page 43	Tiziano Magni
	Colette Masson
	Colette Masson
	Colette Masson
page 44	Colette Masson
page 45	Colette Masson
	Tiziano Magni
	Tiziano Magni
page 46-47	Colette Masson
page 47	Michael Egna

Dancers for The Armitage Ballet:

Jeffery Broadhurst, 1987
Daniel Catanach, 1988-89
Gina DeRicco, 1988
Donna Dunmire, 1988-89
Robin Gardenhire, 1988-89
Robert Gerstner, 1986-87
Corinne Giddings, 1987-89
David Grenke, 1986-88
Victoria Hall, 1987-88
Troy Hoggard, 1988-89
Nora Kimball, 1987-88
Katherine LaNasa, 1986-88
Michael O'Donnell, 1988
Philip Otto, 1986-87
Michael Puleo, 1987-89
Danielle Tiletnick, 1986-88